7.00

ARTHURIAN LEGEND IN THE
SEVENTEENTH CENTURY

JOHNS HOPKINS MONOGRAPHS IN LITERARY HISTORY
III

ARTHURIAN LEGEND IN THE SEVENTEENTH CENTURY

BY

ROBERTA FLORENCE BRINKLEY

1967

OCTAGON BOOKS, INC.
New York

Copyright 1932 by The Johns Hopkins Press

Reprinted 1967
by special arrangement with The Johns Hopkins Press

OCTAGON BOOKS, INC.
175 FIFTH AVENUE
NEW YORK, N. Y. 10010

LIBRARY OF CONGRESS CATALOG CARD NUMBER: 67-18755

Printed in U.S.A. by
NOBLE OFFSET PRINTERS, INC.
NEW YORK 3, N. Y.

TO THE MEMORY OF EDWIN GREENLAW

PREFACE

The study of the Arthurian legend in the seventeenth century has revealed almost no romance. It is the truth of the existence of Arthur and the reality of his great exploits with which those who defend the legend are concerned, for it is the political bearing of the story which is of primary importance. The Stuarts, tracing their descent from Arthur through their Tudor derivation and from the British prince, Llewelin, through their Stuart lineage, continue the Tudor tradition of the use of British material to strengthen and popularize their claims to the throne. When James I antagonized the nation by his insistence upon the Divine Right of Kings, Parliament sought to defend its rights by the support of the ancient Saxon laws. Knowledge of the Saxon language had been lost, however, and the stupendous task of restoring the language called forth the services of the greatest scholars of the age. The study of Saxon resulted in many valuable discoveries. None was of greater importance than the disclosure that the true origin of the nation was Saxon rather than British.

The Tudor emphasis upon the founding of the nation by Brutus and upon the historicity of Arthur made it especially difficult for the political leaders and the historians to overcome belief in these legends. The argument has two phases: the discussion of the Brutus myth, which is acknowledged to be so remote in time that its truth cannot be proved absolutely, and the debate concerning Arthur, whose story belongs to the period in which it should be possible to distinguish between truth and legend. The first line, though intimately bound up with the Trojan-Saxon quarrel, is less closely related to the main body of this study. The detailed account of this part of the controversy has, therefore, been placed in the commentary. Throughout the century the interest oscillated from British to Saxon, according to whether the king or Parliament was in the ascendancy. The evidence for this situation is found chiefly in the political and historical writings of the age, but is supported by corresponding trends in literature. A curious shift in the use of British material comes near the close of the century when Blackmore adapts Geoffrey's story of Arthur to the Revolution in order to show William as the Christian hero overcoming the pagan Saxons, whom he identifies with the Catholics.

The political use of British matter has forced a careful study of the conflict in opinion concerning Arthur found in many minor writers in order that one may fully understand the significance of this controversy for the comprehension of Milton. It has necessitated, also, the adoption of a chronological method of presentation, which results in a sort of anti-climax to the story because of the amusing nature of Blackmore's heavy epics.

I wish to express my appreciation of the Henry E. Johnston Scholarship in The Johns Hopkins University,

PREFACE

1929-30, which made possible this study. I also acknowledge with thanks my indebtedness to the many friends in The Johns Hopkins University and elsewhere who have had a share in this investigation.

R. F. B.

Baltimore, February, 1932

CONTENTS

CHAPTER ONE

The Continuation of the Tudor-British Tradition

Largely through the influence of Malory and Tenny-son the present age thinks of the legend of King Arthur as centered in the Round Table and concerned primarily with the questing of knights, the love of ladies, and the search for the Holy Grail. Arthur seems less real than Lancelot, or Tristram, or Galahad. It is difficult, therefore, for one to realize that there was a period in English thought when the attention was fixed upon Arthur alone, when upon the historicity of Arthur depended the right to the throne of England. This was the period of the Tudors. Tracing their ancestry in a direct line back to King Arthur, the Tudors held that the correct interpretation of Merlin's prophecy concerning the return of King Arthur was to be found not in the actual restoration of the long-awaited Arthur, but in the return of his line. Naturally at a time when the crown was staked upon the existence of Arthur, the king, interest was restricted to Arthur himself; and all such fabulous stories as those of the romances, centering about Arthur's knights—tales which would tend to discredit serious historical facts—, were no longer popular. The Arthurian legend was used by the Tudors in various ways to substantiate their titles to the throne. Henry

VII was the first to see the possibility of political use of prophecy and legend concerning the return of the British. According to a well-known legend, Cadwallader, the last of the British kings, had a vision in which an angel told him that the time had come for the overthrow of the British and that the line should not be restored until after the successive periods of dominion by the Saxons and the Normans. Cadwallader accepted the vision as a divine message, laid aside his crown, and went to Rome, where he devoted himself to a religious life, leaving the country to the inroads of the Saxons. As a descendant of Cadwallader, able to trace his line back to King Arthur, Henry Tudor claimed that the time had come for the completion of the prophecy made to Cadwallader and that through him the restoration of the British was to take place. He came marching triumphantly from Wales under the red-dragon banner of Cadwallader and assumed the English throne in the name of the ancient British. From that time the contention as to whether Arthur, the champion of the British, was a real person or only a fabulous hero had a definite political bearing. To give emphasis to his claims Henry VII named his son Arthur, as Bacon tells us in his *History of Henry VII*, " in honour of the British race, of which himself was . . . according to the name of that ancient worthy King of Briton." Henry VIII, born in Mona, not only held that he was that " sparke of fire" kindled in Mona according to prophecy and therefore the rightful heir to the English crown, but as a descendant of Arthur he also laid claim to territory on the continent won by the reputed conquest of Arthur. It was the prophecy of the return of the golden age with Arthur that Elizabeth turned successfully to her own use to win the confidence of the people in her claims to the throne after the period of war and confusion following the death of Henry VIII. The Arthurian ancestry of Elizabeth was given especial emphasis at the time of her coronation, but its use did not stop there. There was continued interest in the Arthurian-Tudor claim throughout the period, as is revealed by the constant employment of the legend in pageant and entertainment as well as in the historical and literary productions of the age. The sense of security growing up during the age of Elizabeth had its roots in an ancient glorious past, and the leaders of the nation attempted to effect its continuation with an almost intense ardor.

That there must not be a repetition of the crisis in regard to succession which preceded Elizabeth's coming to the throne was one of the dominant political ideas during the long period of Elizabeth's reign. Marriage, therefore, was urged upon the queen by statesman and poet alike and was held to be an obligation to the nation. When there was no longer hope that there would be a royal heir, it became necessary to survey the list of possible successors to the throne in order to try to discover which would cause the least dissension and confusion upon the death of the queen. Claimants to the throne appeared on every hand, and their number and diversity confused the minds of the people. Pamphlets were published, setting forth the titles to the throne of families both in Great Britain and on the continent. In this time of unrest the nation naturally turned to the queen, from whom it had learned to expect decisions even if capricious ones; but Elizabeth steadily refused to name her successor, to express her preference for any one of the possible claimants, or even to allow open discussion of the matter. Such an attitude only augmented the general dissatisfaction. There was particular anxiety lest a change of rulers should cause another civil war or a religious upheaval such as followed the reign of Henry VIII. The dedication of the King James Bible states that the people expected the land to be overshadowed by "thicke and palpable clouds of darknesse." Bacon sums up the situation when he says that other nations, looking upon conditions in England, anticipated

nothing but confusions, interreigns, and perturbations of estate; likely far to exceed the ancient calamities of the civil wars between the houses of Lancaster and York, by how much more the dissensions were like to be more mortal and bloody when foreign competition should be added to domestical, and divisions for religion to matter of title to the crown.

As it became increasingly apparent that the nation was facing a recrudescence of the crisis preceding the accession of Elizabeth, it seemed to many of the nobility that James VI of Scotland was the one person who could avert civil and religious disaster. Accordingly some by secret letters and messengers sought the favor of James; others were so bold as to make their way into Scotland in person. Camden relates that

Puritans, Papists, Ambitious persons and Flatterers of all kinds, and other sorts of men, all of them prompted by their particular Hopes, poasted night and day by Sea and Land into *Scotland,* to adore the rising King, and get into his Favour.

For many reasons James did seem to be the best prospect. He had clear title to the English throne through his great-grandmother, Margaret Tudor, daughter of Henry VII; as a descendant of Henry VII he reaffirmed in his own person the union of the houses of York and Lancaster, a union which implied freedom from civil war; he could be counted upon to give protection to the Protestant religion—a point emphasized in the dedication of the 1611 Bible; and he afforded an opportunity for the continuation of a tradition which had dominated political thought for approximately two centuries and had proved highly successful in a like national crisis.

In preparation for the succession of James, John Harington in his *Tract on the Succession to the Crown* used British material to popularize the claims of James to the throne. He gave two ancient British prophecies concerning the union of Scotland and England and showed how these would be fulfilled in James. He gave especial emphasis to the fact that James was crowned in infancy, and so was to be identified with the babe crowned in the cradle, who, it was prophesied, "shall make the ile of Brutus whole and unparted."

Perhaps nothing which James could offer to the nation had such a tremendous appeal as his power to bring about the long-desired union between England and Scotland. Efforts had been made to accomplish such a conjunction by treaty; when peaceful measures failed, violent ones followed, and what could not be accomplished by agreement was attempted by war. This union had become especially urgent not only in order to balance the power of France but also to counterpoise Spain, which had become united with Portugal under Philip II. In James lay the possibility of the peaceful healing of the division which had caused rancor in the heart of the nation since Brutus first divided the nation among his three sons.

Although the proclamation of James as king of England brought no immediate confusion such as had been anticipated by the watching nations of Europe no less than by the English themselves, James recognized the importance of establishing himself in the Arthurian-Tudor tradition and of associating himself with British prophecy. This was an especially wise and even necessary step in view of the fact that under the will of Henry VIII the Stuarts were excluded from the throne. Naturally he played first upon the note of greatest appeal he could offer the English, the union of the nation; therefore he had himself proclaimed King of Great Britain, giving up his separate titles to the kingdoms. The fact that this union which no previous means could bring about was suddenly accomplished in the natural course of events was one of the chief causes for rejoicing over the accession of James. It was emphasized in the various speeches of welcome made to the king as he came from Edinburgh to London, was celebrated in the entertainments for his reception into London, and was the song of the poets until it gradually became evident that it took more than the proclamation of a king to weld together these nations. But the proclamation itself brought joy not only because of the union it indicated but also because it marked James as the fulfilment of the Merlin prophecy:

Then shall break forth the fountains of Armorica, and they shall be crowned with the diadem of Brutus. Cambria shall be filled with joy; and the oaks of Cornwall shall flourish. The island shall be called by the name of Brutus: and the name given it by foreigners shall be abolished.

Bacon reports that it was commonly believed that prophecy was at last realized in James:

The vulgar conceived that there was now an end given and a consummation to superstitious prophecies (the belief of fools, but the talk sometimes of wise men), and to an ancient tacit expectation which had by tradition been infused and inveterated into men's minds.

The interest in these prophecies and the credit given them are indicated by the editions appearing in the reign of James. There were two editions of the prophecies of

Merlin by Alanus de Insulis in 1603 and 1608, respectively. *The Whole Prophecies of Scotland, England, France, and Denmark. Prophecied by marvellous Merling* was also published in 1603 and again in 1615. In his funeral oration for Queen Elizabeth John Colville pointed out that though the songs of Thomas the Rhymer had once been laughed at, they were now recognized as authentic. James A. H. Murray in his edition of *The Romance and Prophecies of Thomas of Erceldoune* gives several pieces of contemporary evidence to show that belief in the fulfilment of prophecy in James was widespread and that it was a matter of common conversation. He quotes from Archbishop Spottiswood's *History of the Church of Scotland* to show that the prophecy of the union of England and Scotland, the crowning of the child who should bring this to pass, and other such details had been " ratified and made good " through James.

The poets and historians also celebrated this theme. In an historical poem of 1604, called *A Prophesie of Cadwallader,* William Harbert of Glamorgan calls James " The Lords great Stuart . . . our second Brute," who " Shall three in one, and one in three unite." Ben Jonson notes this carrying out of prophecy in his *Masque of Blackness* (1604-5), saying:

> With that great name Britannia, this blest isle
> Hath won her ancient dignity, and style.

It was noted in Thomas Bastard's rare Latin poem to James in 1605 and in other shorter poems. Speed in his summary at the close of his history points out that in spite of superstition and of the prohibition of the use of Merlin's prophecy by the Council of Trent, "Truth bids us acknowledge" that in James is to be found the consummation of the prophecy of both Merlin and Aquila of Shaftsbury to the effect that "the *British Empire* after the *Saxons* and *Normans* should returne againe to her ancient *Stocke* and *Name.*" So it is to James as the "Inlarger and Uniter of the British Empire and Restorer of the British name" that Speed dedicates his history. William Alexander, Earl of Stirling, in addressing his *Monarchicke Tragedies* to King James refers to the consummation of the prophecy, which had been known three hundred years. Drummond in *Forth-Feasting* (1617) recalls that the coming of James had been foretold by "the bards and mysticke Skills" as the time in which "this isle should yet her ancient name regain"; and Slatyer still later in the *Palae-Albion* (1619) celebrates the king crowned "even from a child" who "Brings Peace and Vnion."

The union of the nations which was seen as the accomplishment of British prophecy was also associated directly with Arthur, for under Arthur there had been a period of union even though it was effected by conquest. The Venetian State Secretary, writing on April 17, 1603, states that James "is said to be disposed like that famous and ancient King Arthur to embrace under one name the entire kingdom." James was not only *like* Arthur; he was also considered to *be* Arthur returned to life again through his descendant, or at least to be the successor of Arthur with all that such a claim implied. Campion in his *Masque at Lord Hays Marriage, 1606-7,* expresses the first idea:

> Merlin, the great King Arthur being slaine
> Foretould that he should come to life againe;
> And long time after wield Great Brittaine's State,
> More powerfull ten-fould and more fortunate.
> Prophet, 'tis true, and well we find the same,
> Save only that thou didst mistake the name.

Camden in his *Remaines Concerning Britain* cites the anagram made for King James "declaring his undoubted rightfull claim to the Monarchy of Britain, as the successour of the valorous King Arthur ":

> Charles James Steuart
> Claims Arthur's seat.

Warner in the *Continuance of Albion's England* (1606) allows the return of Arthur in the return of the British name:

And, that your *Arthure* comes againe, so far-forth we allow
It Prophecie, as *Brutaine* dead with him reuiueth now:
That is, *Brutes* Baptisme of this Isle, that ana-baptized grew
By diuers names in diuers parts, *Iames* doth through-out renew.

Ben Jonson in the *Speeches at Prince Henry's Barriers* holds that James is rightful heir to Arthur's seat and compliments the monarch by terming him even greater than Arthur

> Now, when the Island hath regained her fame
> Intire and perfect, in the ancient name,

And that a Monarch equal good and great,
Wise, temperate, just, and stout, claims Arthur's seat.
Did I say equal?   O too prodigal wrong,
Of my o'er-thirsty and unequal tongue!
How brighter far than when our Arthur liv'd,
Are all the glories of this place reviv'd.

In the *Masque of Oberon* (1611) Jonson again terms
the throne "Arthur's chair" and Prince Henry

. . . the proper heir
Designed so long to Arthur's crowns and chair.

The king himself gave emphasis to the idea of his being
like Arthur in his plan to create one thousand knights
"in imitation of King Arthur, who created that number."

Seeing in James the completion of British prophecy
as well as the return of King Arthur, the nation rejoiced
to welcome the new king.   Multitudes thronged to greet
him as he passed through the nation on his way from
Edinburgh to London, so that, as Howes relates in his
continuation of Stow's *Annals,* they were "swarming
in fields, houses, trees, and high wayes, to behold the
king."   Enthusiasm was so high that many unmindful
of their occupations "ran from their carts, leaving their
teams of horses to their owne vnseasonable directions."
That this welcome made a great impression upon King
James is shown in his recollection of it in his speech to
his first Parliament:

Or shall it ever be blotted out of My Mind, how at My first
Entry into this Kingdom, the People of all sorts rid and ran;

nay, rather flew to meet Me? Their Eyes flaming nothing but
Sparkles of Affection, their Mouths and Tongues uttering nothing but Sounds of Joy; their Hands, Feet, and all the rest of
their Members, in their Gestures, discovering passionate Longing and Earnestness to meet and embrace their new Sovereign.

In the magnificent entertainment given in London to
celebrate the arrival and the coronation of the king, it
was the Tudor-British blood of James with its association with Arthur which received continual emphasis.
The " glory of the western world " was said to be
unfolding again in James; he was called the " glorious
stem " of the " Great Monarch of the West " and
praised as the " true-born bud " of Tudor who was " to
sit in Teudor's place." In the Italians' pageant for the
London entertainment King James was represented as
receiving the sceptre from Henry VII, " over both their
heads these words being written,

Hic Vir, Hic Est."

The idea of the return of the golden age, which had
been used effectively by Elizabeth to emphasize the end
of dissension with her accession, was again stressed in
the reception of James, for the gift of peace was one of
the strong claims of James to popularity. Not only had
the acceptance of James by the nation meant an end to
the fear of civil war; it also brought peace to the realm,
for James pardoned Tyrone, thus terminating the
troublesome Irish rebellion, and brought the Spanish
conflict to an immediate end. It was his boast that he

brought peace in his very person, and it soon became evident that he would make whatever sacrifices necessary to preserve peace.   In his " Epistle Dedicatory to the Lord Maior and Aldermen of London " Howes says that

The speedy effecting and establishing of peace in this Kingdome was much more than our neighbour Nations held possible to be so easily performed, as appeared by their great admiration vpon the certain knowledge thereof.

Arthur Wilson in his *History of the Reign of James I* expresses this astonishment by saying that with the advent of the new king it seemed " as if the old Genius of Iron-handed War were departed, and a new one crowned with a Palm of Peace, had taken Possession of the *English* nation."   Roger Coke in writing of the reign of James also stresses the astonishment of " the gazing world abroad."   The emphasis upon this idea helped greatly in popularizing the accession of James, and full advantage was taken of the opportunity to represent in the pageants the return of Astrea and the golden age. The Arch of Triumph above the Conduit on Fleet Street bore a representation of a globe within which

Vpon distinct Ascensions . . . were placed all the States of the land, from the Nobleman to the Ploughman, among whom there was not one word to be heard, for you must imagine as *Virgil* saith:

> Magnus ab integro seclorum nascitur ordo.
> Iam redit et Virgo, redeunt Saturnia regna.

That it was now the Golden world, in which there were few praters.

The Arch of Triumph at Temple-Bar bore a representation of Felicity. She held an outstretched scroll which was inscribed:

Redeunt Saturnia Regna,

out of Virgil, to show that now those golden times were returned again.

In this " golden world " Astrea once more made her home. In the Italians' pageant previously mentioned this idea was symbolized by the figure of Peace lying full length upon the earth. Jonson gave an elaborate representation of the reign of peace in that part of the *King's Entertainment* which he devised for the Temple-Bar pageant. The scene was a temple over which was a Janus head. Beneath the head an inscription showed that now the temple was to be closed, for James brought peace with unity to the realm. Within this temple the first and principal figure was Irene or Peace. By her stood Plutus or Wealth, under whose feet lay Mars " groveling, his armour scattered upon him in several pieces, and sundry sorts of weapons broken about him." Peace was attended by four handmaidens, Quiet, Liberty, Safety, and Felicity, each represented in triumph over her opposite. The Genius of the city explained this display as meaning that James brought

> Sweet peace to sit in that bright state she ought,
> Unbloody, or untroubled; hath forced hence

All tumults, fears, or other dark portents
That might invade weak minds; hath made men see
Once more the face of welome liberty:
And doth in all his present acts restore
That first pure world, made of the better ore.

Electra's speech at the close of the pageant, also by Jonson, recurred to the theme of peace and the " golden reign."

The idea that peace and the golden age returned with James is to be found frequently in the poets, for example: Thomas Greene in *A Poet's Vision, and a Princes Glorie* (1603) rejoiced that virtue which had been confined to the north had once more returned to England, bringing back those days "That ancient Poets long agoe did praise"; Dekker, in telling of the glories attendant upon *The Wonderfull Yeare, 1603*, stressed the return of peace and the golden age, with the benefits resulting to the world of letters and the world of trade; Giles Fletcher in *Christ's Triumph* remarked that other nations " stand to see our peace, as struck with wonderment"; Jonson represented the triumph of the Golden Age over the Iron Age and the descent of Astrea from heaven in the masque at court, *The Golden Age Restored*, and in *Gipsies Metamorphosed* he again praised James for peace; Drummond in *Forth-Feasting* told of the return of the " long-exil'd *Astrea* " and the " Saturnian World " with King James, whose name should surpass the name of Arthur, and in *To the Obsequies of the blessed Prince Iames, King of Great Britain* he spoke of the world which " late was Golden by thy Breath" as turned to Iron; Slatyer in *Palae-Albion* noted that in James "Astrea and Vnion meet "; John Beaumont in *Bosworth Field* expressed delight in the " dayes of peace." This gift of peace was the one thing which the poets could still celebrate, as did Beaumont in *On the Anniversary Day of His Maiesties Reigne Over England,* twenty years after the accession of James. To carry out this idea of the return of peace, James wore no sword at his side when he made his official entrance to the Tower of London, and later in his first speech to Parliament he alluded to the union of the kingdoms as a union " fasten'd and bound up by the Wedding-Ring of *Astrea."*

The Tudor line with its Arthurian claims was not the only line through which James could trace British descent. His ancestry went back to Arthur through the Stuart line also. When Fleance, son of Banquo, escaped the murderers hired by Macbeth, he fled into Wales, where he fell in love with the Princess Nesta, daughter of Griffith ap Llewelin, the last of the native Welsh princes. Their son, Walter, returning to Scotland, became Lord High Steward (whence the name of Stuart) and the ancestor of the Scottish line of kings. The story was said to be " apud Scoto-Britannos cele-brata " and was familiar to the English through Holins-hed's *Chronicles.* Its use in substantiating the claim to the throne was pleasing to both nations, for it employed Scottish history and yet it strengthened the Tudor-

Arthur claims. The double British pedigree of the king was considered so important and of such popular interest that it was displayed upon "two magnificent pyramids seventy feet in height" erected at the Strand for the pageant welcoming James to London. The familiarity with this complex pedigree is testified by the fact that all the plans for the entertainment at the Strand were made and completed in twelve days.

The historical poets kept this double line of British descent fresh in the minds of the people. Warner in 1606 added to his great poem (first published in 1595) the *Continuance of Albion's England,* in which he gave a triple line of British ancestry for James: from Cadwallader through Tudor, from Griffith through Fleance's wife, and from Gladys, wife of Mortimer and sister of Prince David. He also included a *Historie of Macbeth* in compliment to James. Here the Fleance-Nesta story is enlarged by the story of Macbeth and the witches, recounted to Nesta by Fleance, and the prophecy that through Banquo should come a line of kings, which Fleance says must come true through his relations with Nesta. In that part of the *Polyolbion* written after the accession of James, Drayton not only gives the derivation from Margaret Tudor but also refers to the double line of British genealogy when he points out that through Henry Tudor's descendant, "Llewelin's line in him shall doubly thrive," for, as Selden explains in the notes, by the marriage of Henry's daughter of Cadwallader lineage to James IV, of the Nesta-Fleance descent, James I was of British ancestry. William Slatyer, writing his *Palae-Albion* in acknowledged indebtedness to Drayton, whom he calls his master, devotes the Tenth Ode to the story of the Tudors in honor of James, to whom he dedicates his poem. This

> Brings Teudor in, Vnites the Roses,
> Where sprong that Iemme, that ever blest,
> Two factious Realmes in Vnion closes,
> Bryttaines King Iames!

He also relates the story of the escape of Fleance to Wales and traces the descent of James in the Scotch-Welsh line.

The story of the escape of Fleance and of his becoming the source of the Scoto-British succession was incorporated in a dramatic dialogue in Latin prepared by the students of St. John's College in honor of the king's visit to Oxford University in 1605. As the king approached St. John's, three youths dressed as the weird sisters came out to meet him and related the prophecy made to Macbeth that he should be king and that Banquo should be the father of kings. This prophecy is said to be indeed fulfilled, for James is of the race of Banquo:

Vaticinii veritatem rerum eventus comprobavit. *Banchonis* enim e stirpe Potentissimus *Jacobus* oriundus.

Then James is hailed with three hails, the number used by the witches in *Macbeth,* as king of England, king of Scotland, and king of Ireland. This production, " the conceit whereof the king did very much applaude," is thought to have influenced Shakespeare in the composition of *Macbeth*.

That Shakespeare should turn again to history for a dramatic theme attests the popularity of the new line of tradition.   In the days of Elizabeth he had portrayed the union of the houses of York and Lancaster, a Tudor theme.   Now with the accession of the new sovereign he once more turned to history.   The story of Macbeth was most opportune, for it suited the mature powers of the dramatist, while at the same time it afforded a compliment to the king.   Written, it is generally agreed, about 1605-6, certainly after 1603, as is shown by internal evidence, the play shows Macbeth as the medium through which is brought about the fulfilment of the prophecy of the return of the British line to the throne (a reference no contemporary audience would fail to get) and Banquo, from whom the king traced his descent, as the one whose kingly descendants stretched out " to the crack of doom."   The vision of the kings presented to Macbeth by the witches is generally interpreted as showing in the " two-fold balls " the union of England and Scotland under James, and in the " treble sceptres " the union of the entire island as one nation. A. E. Parsons carries the interpretation a step further and sees in the vision of " A child crowned with a tree in his hand " a definite reference to James, who was crowned in his cradle and would " most appropriately bear in his hand a *genealogical tree* showing his descent in double line from the ancient British race."

The consummation of British prophecy in the restoration of the name of Britain, the return of Arthur with its accompanying belief in the descent of Astrea to the earth, and the succession of the line of Banquo to the throne were not, however, the only themes which connected James with early British legend. The theme of union also afforded British material which could be used to compliment James and to popularize his title to the throne, for his ancestral line could be traced back from Arthur to Brute, the legendary settler of the island. A parallel was immediately apparent between Brute, who had first ruled over the undivided kingdom, and James, who once more had secured union and healed the lamented schism brought about by Brutus. In the Arch of Triumph over Fleet Street allegorical figures depicted England, Scotland, France, and Ireland; above the representation it was stated that an Empire was portrayed

By Brute divided, but by you alone
All are again united and made one.

This idea was more fully developed in *The Triumphes of Re-United Britaine* by Anthony Munday, performed by the Merchant Taylors, October 29, 1605. In these *Triumphes* King James is represented as a second Brutus. A preliminary account of the settlement of Britain by Brute and of his division of the country is given. Brute, dressed as a Trojan warrior, tells of the advantages accruing to Britain from the conquest by a civilized race and relates the founding of *Troya-nova* beside the Thames. Three nymphs, representing Leogria, Cambria, and Albania, reprove him for the "hurt and inconvenience" resulting from the division of the kingdom, but are stayed by the fact that they are now "to behold Britaniae's former felicity againe," restored by

our second Brute (Royall King James) . . . by whose happye comming to the Crowne, England, Wales, and Scotland, by the first Brute severed and divided, are in our second Brute re-united and made one happy Britania again. Peace and quietnessse bringing that to passe, which warre nor any other meanes could attaine unto.

Locrine, Camber, and Albanact, "figured there also in their antique estates," do not resent this usurpation of the territory bestowed on them by their father, but "joyfully deliver up theyr Crownes and Sceptres, applauding the day of this long-wisht conjunction." Brute then makes a speech to the effect that the ancient prophecy of union had now been fulfilled, and Troya-nova calls for " Paeans and Songs of Triumph," for Albania

> Hath bred another Brute, that gives againe,
> To Britaine her first name.

The Trojan story was used in entertainment even as late as 1613 when Franckendal, the town which the Palgrave had given to the Princess Elizabeth in jointure, was celebrating the arrival of the Princess. On the second night of her stay there was given a presentation of the Siege of Troy, the event which caused the dispersal of the Trojans and the ultimate settlement in Britain.

The use of the Trojan legend brought about an interesting Roman influence on the vocabulary and thought of the people. For years the mayor was termed *Praetor* and was welcomed by the *senators*. London was Troy, founded by Brutus. The Genius of the city, present when Brutus ran the furrow to lay off the grounds of this Troy, spoke of having seen foretold in " Clotho's book" the happy day of the entry of James, second Brutus, into the city.

It became popular to work out genealogies of James, taking him back at least to Brute, if not to Noah! George Owen Harry in 1604 brought James from Brute to Cadwallader and gave " the worthy descent of his Majesties ancestour, Owen Tudyr." Aubrey, writing the life of Henry Lyte (d. 1607), reports that Lyte " began the genealogy of king James, derived from Brute; which his eldest son Thomas Lyte . . . finished and presented to king James." This was an exceptional piece of work, for it was illustrated with a picture of each king, and it pleased King James so well that he had it engraved and hung it in a prominent place in Whitehall. Anthony Munday in giving an account of it speaks of it as a " seven years labor." Even in dedicatory prefaces may be found detailed genealogical accounts. John Davies, for example, in his Preface to *Microcosmus,* dedicated to Henry, Prince of Wales, begins with Brute and comes through Camber, Brutus's son, to Owen Tudor and thence to Henry.

As the reign of James advanced, the use of British material suffered a noticeable decrease and a decided change in interpretation.   The legendary-historical stories came more and more to be looked upon as the poetic symbol of Wales and Cornwall to be used especially upon the occasion of the creation of the Prince of Wales.   As was explained in a letter to Sir Thomas Campbell, Lord Mayor of London, describing the entertainment, *London's Love to the Prince, 1610*

such representations and misticall understandings have always been reputed lawfull, and are evermore allowed to holde and carrie correspondencie with such solemne shewes and triumphes; as before in elder antiquitie, so likewise in moderne and latter use.

The most elaborate of these representations was that of Ben Jonson in *The Speeches at Prince Henry's Barriers, 1609.*   He pictures the Lady of the Lake as Prince Henry's Fostress, who has bred him " to this hour, and for this throne."   The scene is a lake, near which is Merlin's tomb.   Arthur is discovered " as a Star above " and announces:

> . . . the times are now devolv'd
> That Merlin's mystic prophecies are absolv'd,
> In Britain's name, the union of this Isle,
> And claim both of my sceptre and my style.

He wishes Henry to be as famous as the knights of the Round Table, as Tristram, Tor, Launcelot; and to encourage him in valor Arthur sends down a shield from heaven for him.   Arthur then commands the Lady of the Lake to awake the learned Merlin from the dead that he may instruct Henry, " for Arms and Arts sustain each other's right." She does this with appropriate accompaniments of thunder and lightning, and then presents Prince Henry to him for instruction. Merlin seems to have no difficulty in realizing that it is now the seventeenth century and that the methods of state have changed, and proceeds at once to instruct the Prince in the ideal held by King James that peace is to be preserved at any cost. He points out that the deeds of prowess of the ancient knights " were bold stories of our Arthur's age." The times have changed; he is not to be incited to the deeds

> Of antique Knights, to catch their fellows' steeds
> Or Ladies' palfreys, rescue from the force
> Of a fell giant, or some score to unhorse.
> These were bold stories of our Arthur's age;
> But here are other acts; another stage
> And scene appears; it is not since as then:
> No giants, dwarfs, or monsters here, but Men.
> His arts must be to govern, and give laws
> To peace no less than arms.

Merlin, therefore, presents the history of England, showing first the Tudors and Edward I in order to teach that " laws and trade bring honours in and gain," and that defensive arms bring " safe peace." He then shows a number of reigns in which the disastrous effects of " arms offensive " may be seen. Thus instructed, Henry is considered worthy of becoming the Prince of Wales, and so Merlin awakes Chivalry, who is " Possess'd with

Sleep, dead as a lethargy," and Chivalry brings Knight-hood to the Prince.

Even this poetic usage, however, decreased in popu-larity. When Charles was created Prince of Wales after the death of Prince Henry, the only British material which Jonson used in his *Masque of Pleasure Reconciled to Virtue* is in the anti-masque. The comic Welsh char-acters explain the famous Stuart anagram as meaning " Your madestie s'ud be the first king of Gread Prittan, and sit in Cadier Arthur, which is Arthur's Chair, as by Got's blessing you do." Saying, " We are not here to tauk of Brute," they call for the *British* musicians to come forth and so dismiss the subject.

We find, then, that Arthurian matter, used with the highest political import in the reign of the Tudors and considered of weight at the accession of James, was soon given far less significant treatment as the figura-tive representation of Wales. The decreasing interest in the British was accompanied, as we shall see in the next chapter, by an increasing interest in the Saxons. The underlying causes of this shift form our next sub-ject for investigation.

CHAPTER TWO

THE TROJAN AND THE SAXON ORIGINAL

The acceptance or the rejection of British story in this century was weighted with political import, for it was bound up with the fight between the king and Parliament. The rapid development of interest in the Saxons is attributable to this conflict, which sent the defenders of the rights of the common people to a study of Saxon law. The resulting knowledge of the language revealed through the very derivation of words and particularly of proper names that the Saxon origin of the nation was more plausible than the British. Acquaintance through Saxon writings with the laws and customs of this race confirmed the idea. With the growth of Parliamentary power the attack upon the British became more virulent and developed along two lines: the refutation of the settlement of the country by Brutus and the detraction of Arthur, the greatest British hero. These necessarily included a stand concerning the truth of Geoffrey's *Historia* in which the accounts had their origin. Whenever the king's power prevailed, there was renewed interest in British matter. A study of this situation is absolutely essential for the understanding of Milton's attitude toward the British as revealed in his *History of*

26

Britain and of his rejection of the Arthurian theme for
his epic.

The Change from British to Saxon Interest

Though the feeling of security growing out of the
union of the nation under a " second Brute " brought a
spontaneous outburst of joy at the accession of James,
it was not enough to maintain approbation when it
became evident that the king intended to violate the
fundamental doctrine of the peoples' rights by his insistence upon the Divine Right of Kings. In *The Trew
Law of Free Monarchies or the Reciprock and Mutuall
Duetie Betwixt a Free King and his naturall Subiects* he
set forth points which were diametrically opposed to the
most cherished ideals of English government: the king
is as God; he is subject only to God, and no subject or
law can judge him; it is unlawful for a subject to rebel
against a king—" the wickednesse therefore of the King
can never make them that are ordained to be iudged by
him, to become his Iudges "; he is not subject to the
law, for " the King is above the law, as both the author
and giver of strength thereto "; his power is absolute—
" the King is over-Lord of the whole land: so is he
Master over every person that inhabiteth the same, having power over the life and death of every one of
them "; the coronation oath is not a contract with the
people—" I deny any such contract to be made." Writing on June 26, 1603, the Venetian State Secretary said
that the king " declares that there are no ministers and

no law of which he is not the master." As time passed, the king's claims became more bold and arrogant; and his *Speach to the Lords and Commons of the Parliament at Whitehall,* March 21, 1609, seemed an insult to the nation. In it he stated a doctrine which stripped his subjects of all rights:

Kings are not onely Gods Lieutenants vpon earth, and sit vpon Gods throne, but even by God himselfe they are called Gods . . . they can make and vnmake thair subiects: they have power of raising, and casting downe: of life, and of death: Iudges over all their subiects, and in all causes, and yet accomptable to none but God onely.

Kings, he added, may " make of their subiects like men at the Chesse "; yet the subjects are to make return by " the affection of the soule, and the service of the body." In defense of this absolute power of the king, Dr. Cowell, Regius Professor of Civil Law at Cambridge, wrote *The Interpreter* in 1607. This book stirred the Commons to violent opposition because it not only supported the king's claims but also misrepresented Parliament and spoke " unreverently " of the Common Law. Such great feeling was aroused that it became necessary for the king to suppress the book by Proclamation in 1610. Cowell's *Institutiones* suffered an even worse fate. In its attempt to force the English materials into the Roman pattern it was important as an effort to introduce Civil Law into England. Maitland says that this book " seemed to confirm the suspicion that Roman Law and absolute monarchy went hand in hand." The resentment of the people was so high that the book was " burnt by the common hangman " in 1610.

The growing antagonism toward prerogative brought about an investigation of the constitution of the English government for principles with which to oppose these claims of arbitrary power. The learned Selden in 1616 translated and edited Fortescue's *De Laudibus Legum Angliae* to refute the absolutism of James. Here were stated the principles which opposed point by point the doctrine advanced by the king: the laws are made " by the assent of the whole Realme "; the king is subject " to the observance of his own law," and " cannot alter nor change the laws of his Realme at his pleasure "; the coronation oath is a contract between the king and the people, making the law the arbitrator between them and binding the king to protect his subjects " from his own oppression and extortion, though such willful lusts and necessities do move him to the contrary." These points Selden enlarged and emphasized in his notes.

Selden was one of the most untiring students of the English law which the seventeenth century produced. Jonson called him the " law-book of the Judges of England." In *Analecta Anglo-Britannica* Selden was primarily interested in tracing the legal development of the nation; in *Jani Anglorum Facies* he gave the old laws and customs of the early races; in *England's Epinomis* he gave much of this same material in English; he edited Eadmer's account of the courts of the first two

Williams and of Henry; he wrote concerning the succession in 1631; and finally, he edited *Fleta* in 1647.

The Venetian State Secretary, writing May 12, 1604, reported that Parliament was full of " seditious subjects, turbulent and bold, who talk freely and loudly about the independence and the authority of Parliament in virtue of its ancient Privileges." The revival of such privileges, he says, " will prove a diminution and abasement of the royal prerogative." Raleigh wrote a dialogue in proof of the " prerogative of Parliaments in England," but other publications appeared in support of Divine Right. Aubrey says that Fabian Philips was employed " in searching and writing to assert the king's prerogative." Slatyer, in dedicating the *Genethliacon* to James, supports the idea that kings derive their power directly from God alone and are, therefore, supreme. Such incompatible views held respectively by the king and his subjects incited a study of the origin of English law with the hope of uncovering the fundamental ideas upon which the government rested. Here again the king and the people held opposing views. James argued that English law was from the Normans and dated back only to William the Conqueror:

. . . he gave the Law, and took none, changed the Lawes, inuerted the order of gouernement . . . their old Lawes, which to this day they are ruled by, are written in his language, and not in theirs.

Parliament, on the other hand, vested its claim of

authority upon the " ancient privileges " of the Anglo-Saxon days, for then the people held the prerogative. The question was one demanding the assistance of the antiquaries, and Spelman and Selden especially were indefatigable in their research. Selden's statement in *A Review Appended to the History of Tythes* expresses fully the conclusion to which this inquiry invariably led:

For neither were the laws formerly made, abolished by that conquest, although, by law of war, regularly all rights and laws of the place conquered, be wholly subject to the conqueror's will. For in this of the *Norman,* not only the conqueror's will was not declared, that the former laws should be abrogated . . . but also the ancient and former laws of the kingdom were confirmed by him.

Spelman also showed that it was reasonable for the Conqueror to uphold these ancient laws by pointing out the common origin of the Saxon and Norman races and consequently the fundamental similarity of thought. It was found, in fact, as Selden pointed out, that the very document of the Conqueror's laws bore the inscription, " leges boni regis Edwardi quas Guilielemus bastardus postea confirmavit." That the Magna Charta was only the reaffirmation of the old laws was also stressed, and it was cited that Henry III in ratifying the Magna Charta " granted to the nobility and Commons such *Lawes* and *liberties* as had been used long time before."

Such findings were displeasing to the king, who feared the revival of the ancient privileges and therefore instituted a policy of suppression. The society of antiquaries which had been formed in the preceding century was the first object of the king's displeasure, for it was especially mistrusted on account of the fact that it had published a collection of old laws and was making other investigations of the past. Richard Carew in his *Survey of Cornwall* states that the society was dissolved "lest they should be prosecuted as a cabal against the government." The Latin *Life of Cotton* prefixed to the catalogue of his library narrates that "the King and his Council suspected them of plotting against the state, and when the matter had been thoroughly weighed, the dissolution of the society was imposed, lest it should be the source of plots." When four of the five survivors of the first group, Camden, Cotton, Sir James Ley, and Spelman, attempted to revive the society in 1614, they resolved not to "meddle with matters of State nor Religion," but the king, not learning the self-imposed restrictions, took an immediate dislike to the association, so that only one formal meeting was held.

The king even sought opportunities to withhold from the public the results of the private studies of investigators of the past. Selden, whose legal research had given a solid foundation for the claims of Parliamentary right and the supremacy of common law, was the first one to suffer personal oppression from the king. When the *History of Tythes* was published in 1618, the king held that Selden had "indirectly weakened the claims of divine right" in this study. Reference is made to this effect in Randolph's *Hey for Honesty* when Dull-pate says he dares deny the priests their tithes because

> . . . A learned antiquary
> That has search'd (in)
> The breech of Saturn for antiquities,
> Proves by a reason—an infallible reason,
> With bugle-horn writ in the Saxon tongue,
> That neither praedial nor personal tithes
> Are due *ex jure divino.*

Selden was summoned before the Court of High Commission where " after many threatenings, he was obliged to sign a recantation." This action was termed as disgraceful to England as the proceedings against Galileo were to Italy. The book was suppressed, and Selden was not even allowed to reply to those attacking him. Three years later when he helped the Commons find precedents for its protestation of December 18, he was arrested by the king's orders and put under the custody of the sheriff of London until his trial. Spelman's work also suffered suppression. His comments on the Magna Charta were so much disliked that Laud would not allow that section of the *Glossary* to be printed.

The question of Divine Right had led to the establishment of two opposing camps. The judges, headed by Coke, defended the ultimate authority of the Common Law, and the Ecclesiastical Courts and the universities upheld the supremacy of the king. Coke saw in the Common Law the defense of the people, for the king himself was subject to this law and the judges

were the final administrators of it. The king, however, did not mince words in making clear to the judges
that his powers were "transcendant":

As for the absolute power of the Crown, that is no subject for
the tongue of the lawyer, nor is it lawful to be disputed . . .
it is presumption and high contempt in a subject to dispute
what a King can do, or say that a King cannot do this or that.

By his support of the king and prerogative Bacon
became an opponent as well as a rival of Coke, and the
legal opposition of the two became the most serious
cause of the famous quarrel between the two greatest
lawyers of the age. The clergy argued that the Ecclesiastical Courts held their authority direct from the king
and were, therefore, superior to the Common Law
Courts. Coke, on the other hand, believed that the
Common Law was the supreme authority and that to it
even the king was subject. The dispute between the
two courts was connected with the conflict between the
king and Parliament and was of the highest importance
for the entire question of rights. If the judges of the
Common Law Court could resist successfully the authority of the king, they would demonstrate that they had
the higher power. Their defeat in the well-known case
of the "Commendams" and the dismissal of Coke from
the office of Chief Justice shortly thereafter made it evident that the judges were subservient to the king.

A lighter phase of the combat was the ridicule heaped
upon the Common Law by the universities and answered
by various lawyers, including Coke himself. Cambridge

was enabled to surpass Oxford in entertaining the king by presenting a play entitled *Ignoramus* in ridicule of the Common Law:

Oxford comicke Actours had; Cambridge a lawyer foole,
Who Ignoramus christen'd was by men of her owne schoole:

. . . .

Oxford Acts *in toto* were well pleasinge unto some;
But Ignoramus pleased best the Kinge when it was done.

However that may be, the king enjoyed the play enough to want to see it again; and when the performers refused his invitation to give a performance in London, he returned to Cambridge in May, a fact boasted of in "A Cambridge Madrigal, in Answer to the Oxford Ballad," which was inserted in *Ignoramus* at its second performance to be sung instead of interlude music. The author wrote a new prologue for the second perform- ance and made several additions which pleased the king even more than the first version, so that although the play lasted more than five hours, " his Majesty was much delighted with it and laughed exceedingly; and oftentimes with his hands and by words applauded it." The lawyers replied to this absurd portrayal and biting ridicule with many rhymes and ballads, the very titles of which sufficiently indicate the nature of the content: " To the Comedians of Cambridge,—who in three acts before the King abused the Lawyers with an imposed Ignoramus, in two ridiculous persons, Ignoramus the Master, and Dulman the Clerk,—John a Stile, Student in the Common Law, wisheth a more reverent opinion

of their betters "; or "A modest and temperate Reproof
of the Scholars of Cambridge for slandering Lawyers
with that barbarous and gross title, Ignoramus." Mr.·
Chamberlain wrote Sir Dudley Carleton, May 20, 1615,
that the king's return to Cambridge to see the second
performance of *Ignoramus* " hath so nettled the Lawyers, that they are almost out of all patience, and the
Lord Chief Justice, both openly at the King's Bench,
and in divers other places, hath galled and glanced at
Scholars with much bitterness." Coke had two reasons
to be irate: first, Ignoramus was costumed as Coke
with even his beard cut like Coke's, so that the satire
was very obvious; second, his love of the Common
Law, which he soon sacrificed his position to defend,
was so intense that he resented the slur cast upon it by
the play. The feeling stirred by this play did not soon
die, for in 1617 we find Robert Callis of Gray's Inn
writing *The Case and Argument against Sir Ignoramus
of Cambridge.*

At neither university could one speak against kingly
power. Fuller in his *Worthies* tells how Dr. John Richardson was put down by the king when he was taking
part in the Divinity Act at Cambridge, March 7, 1615,
the year in which Cambridge had delighted the king
with *Ignoramus.* Richardson was citing St. Ambrose's
excommunication of the Emperor Theodosius as an
example in support of excommunicating kings when
King James became angry and said, " Prefecto fuit hoc
Ambrosio insolentissime factum! " Dr. Richardson did

not prolong the argument, but replying: " Responsum vere Regium, et Alexandro dignum! Hoc non est argumenta dissolvere, sed dissecare," he took his seat. At Oxford even a student could not raise the question of the king's power though in the privacy of his own room. When a student at Pembroke inquired of a few friends in his room, " May the king, for breaking fundamental laws be opposed? " he was suspended from all his degrees in consequence. In a sermon at Oxford the opinion was expressed that " if Kings grow unruly and tyrannical, they may be corrected and brought into order by their subjects," but the king had copies of the sermon " publicly burnt by the hangman as heretical " in both " St. Paul's Church-yard and St. Mary's Churchyard, Oxford."

Not satisfied with the negative action of suppression, James adopted a plan for teaching the Divine Right of Kings to the youth of the realm. In a Proclamation of November 8, 1615, he stated that a book entitled *God and the King* had been compiled by his authority for teaching young people " that King James doth rightfully claim whatsoever is required by the Oath of Allegiance." All orders " tending to the Universall publishing and teaching " of this book were confirmed and the "Archbishops etc. have been directed to give order for the teaching of youth in this book." He also published in 1616 and again in 1619 the *Remonstrance for the Right of Kings.*

As the conflict between the king and Parliament grew

more violent, there was so much open expression of rebellion that the king on December 24, 1620, issued a proclamation against the discussion by subjects of matters too high for them. The Parliament of 1620 protested this attitude in no uncertain terms:

The privileges and rights of Parliament are an ancient and indubitable birthright and inheritance of the English, and all important and urgent affairs in Church and State as well as the drawing up of laws and the remedying of abuses, are the proper subjects of the deliberation and resolutions of the Parliament. The members are free to speak upon them in such order as they please, and cannot be called to account for them.

They were called to account, however, for in a letter to be read by the Speaker to the House of Commons James commanded that none "shall henceforth presume to meddle with anything concerning Our Government, or deep Matters of State." The House dared to reply, stating that the king "doth seem to abridge . . . our Ancient and Uudoubted Right, and an Inheritance received from our Ancestors." Enraged, the king publicly tore these protests from the Journal of the House of Commons and dissolved Parliament.

Worn by the struggle to maintain their ancient laws and customs against the royal claim of Divine Right and tired of hearing constantly about the king as God, the people saw the splendid anticipations with which they had welcomed James come to nothing. After all, it was only the "rusty Iron Age," and as such it was represented in the London pageant for 1620. L'Isle expresses the hope, however, that " this iron age " will end when Charles I comes to the throne, and depicts the classical golden age which may be anticipated, wherein even the sheep will wear colored wool. For this study the significance of the disappointment of the people in their monarch and of their fight against the claim of Divine Right is that the nation was drawn from the glamor of an Arthurian dream to the cold practicality of a study of facts which led them into an investigation of the customs and laws of the Saxons.

The struggle between the king and Parliament, necessitating a study of source material, forced a revival of the Anglo-Saxon language. Spelman, Selden, and Coke, the three great figures studying the old laws, realized that to find out the exact nature of the ancient rights and privileges so loudly claimed by Parliament, it was requisite to go back to the Anglo-Saxon documents themselves. These scholars had free access to the vast store of treasures collected by Sir Robert Cotton, but were also interested in acquiring original sources for their own libraries. Coke, for example, had in his private collection seventy-seven law manuscripts, including the " Magna Carta cum statutis," annotated, an illuminated *Secreta Secretorium* " executed for King Edward III before he succeeded to the throne," and a thirteenth century copy of the Saxon laws, which had belonged to Archbishop Parker.

The study of the language in turn substantiated the Saxon origin of English law. When Robert Powell in his discussion of *Leets* stated that the oath of allegiance was first instituted by King Arthur, and when others attempted to draw Parliament from Arthur's time " with successorie continuance untill this Present age," it was Spelman who refuted the ideas. He pointed out that though words common to the related Germanic nations were found in the old laws, there was " not one to my knowledge that riseth from the *British* tongue." He also called attention to the facts that the numerous conquests which the nation had undergone and the practical extinction of the British made it incredible that the British should be the author of laws, and that one may see " what the laws of the Britains were " by inspecting the laws of Hoel Dha, which were " nothing consonant to these of ours at this day, or those of the *Saxons* in times past." William Hakewill, who made a study entitled *The Antiquity of the Laws of this Island* also testifies that " scarce the laws of two nations in the world differ more."

The legal interest of the age was not, however, the only stimulus for a study of Anglo-Saxon documents. The practical results in this field opened the eyes of scholars to the value of primary source material for the understanding of other affairs of their own day, and there soon developed a unified concern in the gigantic undertaking of restoring the lost language, even though the immediate purpose of its revival varied with the particular concern of the investigator. As Bacon had indicated, investigation in one subject illu-

minated other fields. The effort to find out the truth
in regard to the origin and power of English law, for
example, led to a new conception of history as being
" not of Battels and Sieges, Births, Marriages, and
Deaths of Princes, which are temporary and momentary
things, but of the Legal Government of a Nation, strug-
gling with Arbitrary Power and illegal Proceedings."
The old leisurely narrative of the Chronicles did not
suit the growing critical and skeptical attitude, and
there developed an effort to sift material. For the first
time there appeared a sense of the importance of chronology, a definite contribution of seventeenth century
scholarship. Selden saw in chronology the only test for
the truth of history. In the application of such a test
by the historians much of the fabulous and legendary
matter of the chronicles was eliminated. Another step
in advance was through the perception that it was essential to make a study of original sources in order to establish the much-desired authentic past of the nation.
Camden stands at the threshold of this change. Though
he frequently accepted legends as authentic source
material, he realized that he must learn the " British
and Saxon tongues," so that he could use public records,
Ecclesiastical Registers, Acts, Memorials of Churches
and Cities, and other manuscripts. It was also seen to
be necessary to be able to translate old charters, grants
of privilege, and such material. Spelman discovered
that even in the old Latin historians, which were necessary sources, there were " many obsolete terms," which

he soon recognized " must be of pure *Saxon* Original."
Sometimes, indeed, these terms were the key words of
the sentence, so that the meaning of the entire thought
was lost through inability to understand the language.

The argument in regard to translating the Scriptures
into the vernacular, stirred up anew by the authoriza-
tion of James for such a translation, further increased
the interest in the Saxon dialect. The findings of the
sixteenth century antiquaries in regard to the Saxons
having the Bible and other books of divinity in the vulgar were reaffirmed, and this precedent was used to
support the authorized version. It soon became evident
that many of the previous translators " darken the
Scriptures with obscure termes "; others give " partiall
translations and glosses "; and a third type " stuffe the
text with such fustian, such inkehorne termes, as may
seeme to favour their parts; or darken at least the true
meaning of holy Scripture, and discourage weake readers with doubtfull sense and harshnesse." To get rid of
such errors it was essential to compare the Anglo-
Saxon text of the Scriptures with the translation.

William L'Isle in the preface of his *Anglo-Saxon
Treatise* gives a good summary of the lines of interest
which had developed. The reasons for the study of
Anglo-Saxon, he says, are: " To vnderstand the right
meaning of our old lawes, which often giue light to the
new "; to find the true meaning of titles, charters, privileges, and territories; to correct faulty translations of
the Scriptures; " to finde out . . . Etymologies and roots

of our words and names now vsed: which many not knowing, doe much mistake "; to decide controversies among Heralds and antiquaries. The purposes of the investigation were practical and immediate, in the spirit which Bacon had suggested in the *Advancement of Learning,* when he set forth the need for the " connecting and transferring the observations of one art to the uses of another," so that the knowledge of the whole past might be used in the administration of affairs in the present. Selden gives an unqualified statement of just such a purpose in research in the dedication of his *History of Tythes* to Sir Robert Cotton, saying that it gives " necessary light to the present in matter of state, law, history, and the understanding of good authors," so that the present has the knowledge of experience " as if we had lived even from the beginning of time." It is this attitude toward antiquity which William Cartwright praises in his poem *To the Memory of the Most Worthy Sir Henry Spelman* when he says:

> Thou didst consult the Ancients and their Writ,
> To guard the Truth, not exercise the Wit.

Bacon and Selden both had little patience with the type of research which had been the interest of the Elizabethan Society of Antiquaries. Archbishop Parker, the founder of the society, had undertaken a practical but narrow field of research in his defense of the Anglican establishment by reference to old authorities. Jocelin in his preface to Parker's *Antiquities* speaks of Parker's " diligent search for such writings of historye, and other

monumentes of antiquitie, as might reveale vnto vs what
hath ben the state of our church in England from tyme
to tyme." His great passion was that of the collector.
For the finding and preservation of old manuscripts
all scholars owe him a debt of gratitude. His associates
were men largely interested in antiquity for its own
sake, archeologists, collectors and students of old coins
and relics, or collectors and editors of old manuscripts.
Bacon held that this type of work was merely " to
derive honor and pomp to learning, . . . to gratify an
eager curiosity and fondness of knowing and preserving whatever may relate thereto," and so missed the
true aim of the study of the past. Selden felt that the
" too studious affectation of bare and sterile antiquity "
was " to be exceedingly busy about nothing " and " may
soon descend to a dotage." Antiquity which shows
merely " what hath been " he termed the " steril part
of antiquity," which he valued slightly. In his *History*
Milton also slurred at the antiquarians " who take
pleasure to be all their lifetime, raking in the Founda-
tions of old Abbies and Cathedrals." Earle characterized
the antiquary as one who " loves all things the better for
being moldy and worm-eaten," admires " the rust of
old monuments," seeks ruined abbeys, and collects coins
and relics. He is more enamored of the past than the
present and " hath more pictures of Caesar than James
or Elizabeth." Milton considered this type of antiquarians as " hinderers of reformation " and used the term
antiquarians for them in contrast with *antiquaries,*

" whose labors are useful and laudable." But anti-
quarianism such as Earle described was one of the ways
of escape in the seventeenth century from the philosophical questioning and political strife which led many
of the best minds to immerse themselves in such interests as bore fruit in the *Hydriotaphia* or *The Anatomy
of Melancholy,* but helped to solve no immediate prob-
lem. Of like nature were the intellectual groups which,
retired and aloof from the main stream of events, met
together at Great Tew to consider religious questions
or at Gresham College to delve into scholarly inquiries.

The intellectual giants of the age, however, engaged
their strength in the service of progress.   Steeves terms
the century a "barren period for the productive study
of the literature of English antiquity "; such study was
not the first aim of the investigators. The new aim was
not the preservation of the relics of the past but an
investigation of the thought and customs of a former
time for their value in settling contemporary problems.
The first step of the scholars was, therefore, translation
and paraphrase; any extensive reprinting of the text
was necessarily a later step. The tremendous rise of
interest in the language during the century is, however,
shown by a survey of such bibliographies as give the
printed volumes which include material in the original,
Wülker's, or Kennedy's, or Miss Eleanor Adams's.

It is difficult for us today to realize the "incredible
labor " of those giants, Cotton, Spelman, Selden, L'Isle,
Whelock, D'Ewes, Dugdale, Twysden, Ussher, and the

other " English Varros," who undertook to unearth this
material for which there was such urgent need, from
the libraries of both individuals and institutions where
it lay " like a treasure hid, to no vse," and to restore the
knowledge of the language in which it was written.
The patiently acquired knowledge of the Saxon won by
Archbishop Parker and his group in the preceding century had been completely lost, for no dictionaries had
been printed or grammars made to preserve their findings. Had Lawrence Noel been more industrious in
the study of words, or Jocelin listened to Parker's impor-
tunity to complete his collection, the scholars of the
seventeenth century would have had something upon
which to begin their work. As it was, however, these
later scholars had to find a method of work before they
could hope for progress. White Kennett in the life of
Somner prefixed to the latter's *Treatise of the Roman
Ports and Forts in Kent* says that the " Saxon language
was extinct, and the monuments of it so few and so
latent, that it requir'd infinite courage and patience, to
attempt and prosecute the knowledge of it." Spelman
and L'Isle give us insight into the methods which they
employed. Spelman compares the struggle to a combat:
his arms are books—the Church Fathers, the laws, the
historians of the Middle Ages, and whatever pertained
to antiquity—and he descends into the arena where
strange words from all sides rush together, almost
impossible to overcome. His method of establishing a
meaning for these unknown words was to collect many

instances of their use and compare the passages in which they occurred. By this means he ultimately arrived at a definition. The result of his colossal undertaking was his *Glossary,* published 1626 to 1664, which was of the greatest service to succeeding students of antiquity. L'Isle first studied both high and low Dutch, then read " for recreation " in old English, whether poetry or prose. He soon saw that his understanding was in direct ratio to the age of the language, for the older it was, the more nearly it approached the Saxon. By means of his knowledge of Latin he was able to follow Virgil " Scotished " by Gawain Douglas, which being " neerer the Saxon, because farther from the Norman," he found to be more help than anything else. Finally, he read the decalogue " set out by Fraerus in common character, and so prepared to come to the proper Saxon," in which at first he was able to read only matter familiar in content. As his ability increased, however, he was able to venture further and further from the known. Other great figures in the early part of the century were also at work upon the restoration of the language. Camden's work is given in the *Remaines* (1605), in which there are a study of the derivation of names and surnames, chapters on the Saxon language, and a chronological series of versions of the Lord's Prayer, which afforded both a plan and elementary material for the study of the development of the language. His interest in the original Saxon is further shown by the fact that in the *Collection of Historians,* published in 1603, he had already reprinted King Alfred's Anglo-Saxon preface to Gregory's *Pastoral Care*. That his *Remaines* proved to be a popular and useful work is testified by the fact that there were seven or eight editions before 1674. Verstegen, " by studie and travaile," was able to write of the customs, laws, and language of the Saxons, and to make a collection of some four or five hundred Saxon words, a list used by Somner in the first dictionary, 1659. His book also ran into a number of editions —five before 1673. The first Anglo-Saxon dictionary, though bearing the name of Somner, was the work of many men. It incorporated a number of previous attempts of a similar nature which had remained in manuscript, as well as much material secured from personal friends. The need for such a work had long been felt, and Lawrence Noel in the preceding century had done pioneer work in the field. Jocelin had also made a collection of words, which had remained incomplete and unpublished. William L'Isle was working on a dictionary in 1631 when Sir Simonds D'Ewes, hearing that he intended to publish it, gave up making his own compilation. Spelman was particularly anxious that a dictionary be compiled by an Englishman, and when Johannes de Laet of Leyden corresponded with him concerning a dictionary, he wrote to Whelock that he was not " willing it should be done by a stranger, and we here (to whome it more particularly belongeth) be pretermitted." Meric Casaubon thought Somner the man for the work and tells in *De Quatuor Linguis* of how he

" ceased not then to importune him that he would think
of compiling a Saxon Dictionary." For a time, however,
Somner was not involved in the work, for as the years
passed and L'Isle's work did not appear, D'Ewes
resumed his work, encouraged in it by de Laet and
Casaubon. Finally, January 2, 1650, Dugdale wrote ask-
ing him not to neglect " this opportunity of Mr. Sum-
ner's helpe " to " speede ye impression of your Saxon
Lexicon and the Laws," and in March before D'Ewes's
death the following month we have the testimony of
Dodsworth that the dictionary " is finished by Mr. Sum-
ner's hand," a fact that seems generally to have been
overlooked. After the death of D'Ewes, Somner spent a
number of years enlarging and perfecting this work. In
1656 we find him writing to Dugdale, " Be mindfull of
me (I beseech you) as to Mr. Laet's Dictionary, wch I
much long to see." Not only this but also Aelfric's
Glossary, transcribed by Junius from a copy in the
library of Peter Paul Rubens at Brussels, was sent to
him. Selden sent him Noel's glossary; Jocelin's had
previously been used by D'Ewes as had also Dugdale's
own manuscript dictionary. L'Isle's manuscript dictionary and other smaller lists were made available for him.
The generosity of such friends and his own material
" magna diligentia collecta " enabled him to produce,
nine years after the death of D'Ewes, a work which was
hailed as epochal. He was called the " great Restorer of
the Saxon Tongue," the one who had made the use of
foreign terms no longer necessary:

   . . . wee'l now forget
Our female *French*, and *Norman* Sibbolet.
Hence *Moot; Vous-avez* hence; for now we heare
Our Lawes with an intelligible Eare.

This dictionary made the language seem far less formidable, so that one could venture back to " the Fountain-Head " and study " the Dark *Meanders* of those *Ages* past . . . with far more Ease and haste."

Following Somner, others published etymological studies, but it was not until 1689 that the first Anglo-Saxon grammar was published. After this new tool was given for understanding the language, it was felt " that now to be ignorant of that Tongue is not the misfortune of a Scholar, but his fault."

The story of seventeenth century scholarship is a thrilling one of patience and ingenuity, of coöperation, and of days in which thirteen and fourteen hours were spent in study. Such enthusiasm is still a challenge. One away from London writes that to think of Sir Robert Cotton's library " sets my mouth to watering "; another feels that a person will be repaid for undertaking almost insurmountable difficulties, for " the discoveries he will find himself able to make in these things will be so delightful to him, that he will scarce be sensible of his pains "; a third speaks of the " sacred ambition in the spirit of Learning, that will not let a man rest without new conquests, and enlarg'd dominions . . . the wishes are those of the Eastern Monarch, to have more than one old world to bring into subjection." L'Isle felt that to neglect the language was a " foule disgrace," both because of the ignorance resulting and because of the " extreme ingratitude " shown " toward our famous ancestors, who left vs so many, so goodly monuments in this their old Dialect recorded." One of the most charming of the later seventeenth century anecdotes relates that a prayer of Hearne's preserved among his papers in the Bodleian tells of a " signal instance " of God's providence the preceding day, " when I unexpectedly met with three old MSS. for which, in a particular manner, I return my thanks." This is the adventuresome spirit of the knights of the Middle Ages or of the voyagers of the Renaissance.

The increasing study of the Saxon led to a growing appreciation of the language for its own sake as well as for its practical value in enabling one to read important documents in the original. There soon arose a feeling of pride that the Saxons " preserv'd entire their primitive language." Verstegen points out the " propriety, worthiness, and amplitude thereof," and both Camden and L'Isle come to the conclusion that it is a pity that the nation had adopted the course of " base and beggarly borrowing " of these " forraine words," since " we have forgot better of our owne." Spelman recognized the Anglo-Saxon as the true and genuine English language, felt that in so far as the present English had departed from the old Saxon it had degenerated from its native purity, and maintained that in order to understand the contemporary language it was necessary to comprehend the original Saxon. The clearness and conciseness of the language were also recognized. L'Isle in singing the praises of the old Saxon says:

For what tongue is able more shortly and with lesse doubtfulnesse, to give vtterance and make way for the cumbersome conceits of our minde, than ours? What more plentifull, than ours might be, if we did vse well but our owne garbes, and the words and speeches of our sundry shires and countries in this Iland? Neither is it the least glory of a Nation to haue such a language.

John Beaumont in writing concerning the *True Form of English Poetry,* comments upon the usefulness of Saxon words in completing the line of verse; Richard Carew writes *An Epistle Concerning the Excellency of the English Tongue;* and near the end of the century, Sir Thomas Browne writes a tract in praise of the Saxon language.

Saxon names had been praised in former times because they expressed " nature's selfe "; John Wilkins saw the possibility of formulating a universal language upon such a foundation, basing each word upon the nature of the thing for which the word was a symbol. He thought that such a language would correct many errors which had originated through misinterpretation of terms or through differing interpretation of them. He spoke especially of " unmasking many wild errors, that shelter themselves under the disguise of affected

phrases," and felt assured that the philosophical examination of " several of those pretended, mysterious, profound notions, expressed in great swelling words" would
reduce them to " nonsense" or show them to be " very
flat and jejune." Realizing that " many impostures and
cheats " were carried on " under the disguise of affected
insignificant phrases," Wilkins devoted great time and
labor to a study of the language.

Less than a century saw the revival of interest in a
forgotten language, the working out of a method for
determining the meaning of words, and the development of an appreciation of the language itself. The
movement had its beginning in the defense of the
people against the Divine Right claimed by the king
and broadened out into other fields in which the practical need for research threw the inquirers back upon
Saxon documents. The results, however, were more than
utilitarian; they revealed to the nation through custom,
thought, and language that the British derivation with
all the romance of Uther's son was a hollow myth and
that the Saxon original was the only trustworthy source
for the race. Camden had led the way in suggesting the
more probable derivation of the nation from the Gauls,
but he would not absolutely deny the Trojan legend
since he felt that such an origin might be an incentive
to the nation and since it had been so long accepted as
true that " absolutely to reject it would be to make war
against time and to fight against receiv'd opinion." The
study of the Anglo-Saxon language and the investiga-

tion of the etymology of words substantiated the Teutonic origin of the nation, for they showed the language to be one with the Gothic and its branches on the continent. Spelman in his preface to the *Glossary* states that his study convinces him concerning the true source of the nation:

Video et nosmetipsos a Gothis late Europam opprimentibus, originem duxisse; moresque et leges aliquot cum vocabulis multis nondum exoletis, imbibisse.

The greater number of place names were also discovered to be Saxon, for the conquering Saxons had given new names to places and the British names had been forgotten. The suitability and expressiveness of the Saxon name had preserved it through succeeding conquests. This proves, says L'Isle, that " our Saxon Ancestors were a very wise and vnderstanding people, and had a very significant and composable tongue." The etymology of both Christian and surnames also revealed an astounding number of Saxon names and showed the origin of families, as Verstegen pointed out in a chapter entitled, " How, by the Surnames of the Families of England, it may be discerned from whence they take their original, to wit, whether from the ancient English Saxons, or from the Danes and Normans." He gives a list of Saxon proper names to emphasize the point. Camden, in the *Remaines,* also gives such a list, doubting if any in his age " will prove like the Gentleman, who distrusting our names, preferred King Arthur's Age before ours, for the gallant, brave, and stately names then used." The study of family names aroused a new interest in genealogy, and the tracing back of genealogy in turn confirmed the Saxon ancestry.

THE CONFLICT CONCERNING THE ORIGIN OF THE RACE

In spite of the convincing nature of the evidence presented by scholars for the Saxon origin of the English, the Brutus myth was not to be given up without a struggle. There arose a century-long debate as to whether the Trojan or the Saxon origin of the race were the more true and noble. The subject was of such general interest that even among the actors, according to Heywood's *Apologie for Actors,* there was hardly a one in the time of King James who could not " discourse of any notable thing recorded even from William the Conqueror, nay, from the landing of Brute until this day."

One of the most curious aspects of this struggle was the effort to establish a Saxon line for the very king whose double British ancestry had been so fully noticed and against whom the Saxon material had been revived. There is no doubt that the Union of the nations under James played a part in originating this idea, for in order to strengthen the feeling of unity, it was shown that the king himself represented the fusion of the races which made up the united kingdom. It was recognized that " in his Person was reconciled all the Titles of our *Saxon, Danish,* and *Norman* Race of Kings," and elaborate genealogies were worked out to prove the point. Warner in his *Continuance of Albion's England* mentions that " *Brittish, English, Scottish,* and the *Danish* bloods vnite In *England's* royall Issue." Though in tracing the full genealogy of James in *Genethliacon sive Stemma Jacobi,* Slatyer shows the same British sympathy evident in the *Palae-Albion* to which it is supplementary, he also incorporates the complex interrelations with the other races. Apparently he used the old genealogies of the British bards in formulating the tables which show how the line went back from Brutus to Aeneas, to Noah, and to Adam; and as the complete title shows, his primary object was to give the descent of James in this line through both the Tudor and the Scottish descent. Yet to complete the genealogy, Slatyer also works out the Saxon, Danish, and Norman lines, taking James back through Lord Darnley to Malcolm and Margaret and so eventually to Fargus and Ethelred, and connecting him with the Danes through the daughter of King Christian, and the Normans through Henry Beauclerc. The details of this descent were so well known that as late as 1660 the author of the *Royal Oak,* a pageant performed by the Merchant Taylors, is able to explain it in full. To Slatyer it appears that if you carry a genealogy far enough it makes the whole world kin, so that the British monarch is related to the royal blood of most of the continent:

> You see how *French, Dutch, English, Danish, Spaines, Greeke,* and more blouds, spring in the Princely Ueines:

Most Princes that weare *Europes* Diadems,
May from your grace derive their Royall Stemmes;
Here Mortall fiend's allai'd, Roses Combin'd,
Strange severall *Nations*, and whole *Kingdomes* joyn'd.

William L'Isle, however, refers with pride to King James as "my soueraigne Lord and Master, so descended as he is, of Britan, Saxon, Scottish, and Norman bloud Royall." Though he claims ancestry from Brute for Prince Charles, in fulfilment of the Eagle's prophecy, he points out that Charles is " our chiefe Saxon name " and that the use by the Prince of a Saxon emblem indicates that Charles will defend "our ancient Dialect" from the " throat of time." John Beaumont writes of James as one who unites the " Britan, English, Norman, Scottish lines." Verstegen, the militant aggressor for the Saxons, is far more daring. Ignoring the British descent of James entirely and claiming that the English are not even a mixed nation, since the coming in of the Danes and Normans meant only the reunion of races which " had one same language and one same originall with us," he boldly dedicates his defense of the Saxon original for the race to King James, " descended of the chiefest blood-Royall of our ancient English-Saxon Kings."

Verstegen is, indeed, the first to show an unreserved admiration for the Saxons and to write a systematic argument to prove that the English derive from them. He feels that through the Tudor emphasis upon the

British, the nation has forgotten its true original. The title of his book sets forth charmingly the task which he appointed himself: *A Restitution of Decayed Intelligence in Antiquities, concerning the most noble and renowned English Nation.* It is of the greatest importance, he explains in the " Epistle to Our Nation," to clear the confusion between the British and the English, especially in view of the fact that "divers of our English writers have beene as laborious, and serious in their discourses of the Antiquity of the Brittains as if they properly appertained unto Englishmen, which in no wise they do or can do, for that their of-springs and descents are wholly different." The Saxons are the " owne truer, and meere Ancestors " for the English:

Englishmen cannot but from Saxon originall derive their descent, and ofspring, and can lacke no honor to be descended of so honourable a race, and therefore are the more in honour to know and acknowledge such their owne honourable and true descent.

Such descent from " so great, so antient, and so honourable a people as the Gaules " surpasses seeking ancestry in the times of the British where there is " unlikely-hood of truth." Their correct ancestry makes it unnecessary for them to lay claim to British honors, " not needing to borrow it of any in the world "; and since such claims serve only to make them ridiculous in the eyes of the British, they should be abandoned. He considers that British ancestry has been highly over-rated and holds it no honor to seek an origin from " the poore miserable fugitives of a destroyed City."

Verstegen is not the only writer who suggests that Saxon ancestry is more honorable than British. Speed says concerning the British genealogy, " their Brute . . . cloudeth their glory in the murders of his parents, and imbaseth their descents, as sprung from *Venus* that lascivious Adulteresse." In writing the note upon Drayton's plea that it is much better to trace descent from " Gods, and Heroes old " than from the " Scythian poore " (by whom Drayton means the Saxons), Selden takes the position that Saxon ancestry is not to be scorned, for it is

as noble and worthy a nation as any red of ; and such a one as the *English* and others might be proud to derive themselves from, as any which do search for their ancestors glory in *Troian* ashes.

The Scythians as well as the British, he says, may trace their source back to the gods and heroes of old, and they have " honorable allegories " as impressive as those of any other race. In addition to these honors they also have men of learning, a distinction which would make an especial appeal in the reign of James. Selden, in fact, rejects the story of the founding of the nation by Brutus except in a " poetical way." In the notes on Fortescue he makes a still stronger denial of the legend, saying, " I see not why any, but one that is too prodigal of his faith, should believe it more then Poeticall story, which is all one (for the most part) with a fiction." If the nation will not give up a Trojan origin altogether, he shows that a much more trustworthy line of descent could be found in the marriage of the British with the Roman colonists. This Trojan legend would be more authentic if it existed in any of the classical writers, but it was originated by Geoffrey, whose account is " much suspected in much reicted." Selden, in spite of his own view, offers the evidence for Geoffrey's position and tells of the general acceptance of this material. Though Geoffrey has " stuft himselfe " with " infinit Fables and grosse absurdities," such stories are followed " with sufficient iustification by the Muse." He suggests the " difference of time " as the " most excellent note to examine truth of historie by " and sees that chronology before the first recorders was a mere pretense to be believed as Ariosto, "Spenser's Elfin Story," or Rabelais. He recognizes that it is only after the coming of Caesar that we have more than conjecture, and in his *Analecta Anglo-Britannica* of 1615 he treats the period before Caesar as frankly fictitious. As did Milton a half century later, he considers the legendary stories " non male tamen si poetice " and gives them " succincte collecta." In making the distinction between the material which may be true for poets and that which can be accepted by historians, Selden is taking an advanced step in regard to national legends. John Taylor, the Water-poet, relates that many writers feel that the British origin of the race may not be accepted without positive dishonor to the nation, for it means deriving the race " from a Paracide, and one that derived his descent from the Goddess (alias strumpet) Venus."

In the long debate concerning the proper original for the nation, Camden's opinion was so highly respected and so often quoted by succeeding historical writers that it must be taken into consideration throughout the seventeenth century. William Nicolson, looking back over the century in 1696, says that Camden has been to the writers concerning ancient times as " *Homer* was of old to the Poets of *Greece.*" The demand for Camden is testified by the appearance of the folio edition of the *Britannia* in 1607 and of the English translations in 1610, 1637, and 1695, respectively. Camden quotes the critics of the legend, and is himself tolerant but dubious. His broad learning had shown him that the desire to derive from the Trojans was a convention common to all European nations: as France had her Francio or Denmark her Danus, so Britain had her Brute. Other nations were giving up these fabulous origins and there was " much wonder why the *Britains* should so fondly adhere to their *Brutus.*" The early days, he says, were uncivilized and without learning, the reports of the Bards and Druids were oral, and there remains no certainty of fact; the stories of the origins of the nations have been invented to fill the gaps, " everyone according to the strength of his own imagination," so that it is doubtful if truth can ever be sifted from invention in those earliest times. He thinks, however, that the more reasonable origin is from the Gauls. He does not contradict the Brutus origin, for, "Absolutely to reject it, would be to make war against time, and to fight against a receiv'd opinion." The number who follow Camden in their general line of argument is practically double the number who defend the Brutus myth without qualifications. The roll of those doubtful of the myth or definitely rejecting it bears such names as Speed, Selden, Raleigh, Bolton, Daniel, Milton, Stillingfleet, and Temple, while the most distinguished name which the latter group can boast is that of Drayton.

THE CLASH OF OPINION IN REGARD TO ARTHUR

Whatever the stand taken toward the early British period, there was still the period after the Roman invasion to be reckoned with, and this interval included Arthur about whom the interest of the sixteenth century had centered. It followed the Roman period, which the historians generally accepted as the beginning of authentic records, and therefore was of more serious importance even from the point of view of chronological history alone than was the story of the founding of the nation.

In writing of "The Arthurian Material in the Chronicles," Fletcher says that with the development of history in the seventeenth century there was little continued interest in Arthur, and A. E. Curdy speaks of the "sudden decline in interest," which he calls "amazing" and for which he says "there is no direct testimony as to the cause." A detailed study of the century, however,

reveals that the Arthurian legend was closely inter-
woven with the political affairs of the entire century,
that it was supported by the loyalists and refuted by the
Parliamentarians with more depth of feeling than is
usually awarded legendary matter, and that the decline
in interest is in direct ratio to the supremacy of Parliament and the interest in the Saxons. As one would
expect in this case, the chief expressions of interest are
to be found in the antiquaries, the historical writers,
whether poets or historians, and the lawyers. The literature reflects the political attitude and is concerned
primarily with Arthur's great deeds and continental conquests; there is almost no romance. Since the source for
this material was Geoffrey's *Historia,* the conflict naturally centered in Geoffrey's reliability and became more
violent than the dispute over the Trojan origin, which
was really only a subordinate part of this major contention.

In the early years of the century the Society of Antiquaries lent its influence to the support of Arthurian
details. The members studied such topics as the manner
of Arthur's burial, his tomb, his epitaph, the Round
Table preserved at Winchester, and the arms of Arthur's
knights. Camden, standing at the threshold of the century, voices the mistrust of men of learning in Geoffrey.
He feels that Geoffrey's British sources, which he
accepts as real, are themselves only fictions and that to
these Geoffrey adds his inventions and other forged
material. Whenever Camden finds Arthur associated

with some place which he mentions, he carefully gives his source of information. He accepts Arthur as a " strong bulwark of the British government " and says that it is " amongst his greatest misfortunes, that the age did not afford a Panegyrist equal to his Virtues."

It is only natural that writers strongly steeped in the Tudor spirit should continue their interest in Arthur upon the accession of a new sovereign who himself gave emphasis to his British descent. It seems significant that Richard Nicols in the 1610 edition of the *Mirror for Magistrates* should include accounts of both Queen Elizabeth and King Arthur. Though the former is probably dated 1603, we have no other date for the section on Arthur than the date of publication. The account continues the Tudor conception of the legend and has the definite purpose of refuting with the true facts Arthur's " corrupted storie, Defac'd by fleeting times inconstant pen," in order to combat the growing skeptical attitude. The ghost of Arthur is called up to tell his own story, which is given in great detail, following Geoffrey's account with extreme closeness except that all suspicion of Arthur's bastardy is refuted.

An early historical manuscript, *Sloane 1090,* gives unquestioned a brief account of Arthur. Speed in 1611 developed a method of historical study which enabled him to reach more definite conclusions than his predecessors concerning the reliability of early history. He summarizes points from various sources, leans heavily on classical authority, tries to account for the omission or inclusion of certain stories, and applies the test of chronology which he calls " the onely *touch-stone* to the truth of histories." He argues that the very existence of fables denotes a foundation of truth, and so accepts the existence of Arthur, though he thinks him of Roman blood, and the general outline of the Arthurian story. He does, though, reject the more romantic points, merely referring the reader to their sources:

Of Arthur's successe both at home and abroad, his great magnificence in *Court* and *Country,* his *Banners,* and foure *Golden Swords* borne before him, his *Round Tables,* and challenges *of Martiall Honour* let *Monmouth the Writer, Newbery* the Resister, and *Leiland* the Maintainer, bee heard for me.

He believes that Geoffrey was " well skilled in *Antiquities* of tradition," but has added to these " out of his owne braine " until he has discredited the hero he meant to magnify. The conquests of Russia, Lapland, and Norway, Speed considers among the fabulous additions which have " made not onely his Acts to be doubted of, but even his person to be called in question, whether any such *Arthure* ever ruled in *Britaine.*" Anthony Munday merely gives a brief summary of the deeds of Arthur without taking sides in the contest over the truth of the material. Samuel Daniel in his *Collection of the History of England* regrets the disbelief in Arthur that has arisen and holds that Arthur was " worthy to have been a subject of truth to posterity, and not of fiction (as Legendary Writers have made him)."

With a desire originally born of the patriotic fervor of Elizabethan days to glorify the nation, Drayton had conceived the plan of writing a leisurely itinerary of the realm, enriching the interest of each place by narrating its historical or legendary associations. In the reign of James there was real need for continuing this work, for England seemed to be forgetting her past, a thing which Drayton thinks is endangering her prestige among other nations, and the people have come to prefer " the fantasies of forraine inuentions " to " the Rarities and Historie of their owne Country, deliuered by a true and native Muse." To one who loved " all brave and ancient things " such a state was intolerable. The critics, he says, are too severe:

> And he the brauest man who most can contradict
> That which decrepit Age (which forced is to leane
> Vpon Tradition) tells; esteeming it so meane,
> As they it quite reiect, and for some trifling thing
> (Which Time hath pind to Truth) they all away will fling.

He inveighs bitterly against those who would discard as false the whole story of Arthur just because some " fictive ornament " has crept in. The age is like that of Henry II when

> Ignorance had brought the world to such a pass
> As now, which scarce beleeues that *Arthur* euer was.

He refutes those who argue against Geoffrey and makes a paraphrase of his account for the song of the

Welsh nymphs in their dispute with the Saxon nymphs over the Island of Lundy. He also makes use of the Arthurian associations with the various rivers and towns. In the First Song when he tells of the river Camell, he recalls that it flows near Arthur's birthplace and that it was on her bounds that Arthur's last battle took place. It is Arthur's blood that made the river so " frantick " that in her grief she twists and turns, making a tortuous course. In the Third Song Drayton comes in his tour to the renowned Camelot, which he associates with the Round Table and the " sports at Pentecost," and to Glastonbury where Arthur's tomb was found, to the great amazement and conviction of all those as skeptical as the people of Drayton's own day. In the Fourth and Fifth Songs, respectively, there are the complete story of Arthur and his achievements sung by the Welsh nymphs and Sabrina's prophecy of the return of Arthur's line to the throne in the return of the British line to which, as we have seen, James doubly belongs. The Severn sings in the Eighth Song of the derivation from Brute:

> Out of whose ancient race, that warlike *Arthur* sprong;
> Whose most renowned Acts shall sounded be as long
> As *Britains* name is known.

The Ninth Song gives the story of the British princes in Wales, stressing their prowess. Part II begins with an account of the famous voyages by sea made by the English. Following Hakluyt, Drayton makes Arthur the first of the " Argonauts " because of his invasion of Norway, Greenland, and Lapland. Finally, in the Thirtieth Song Cumberland boasts of the mound named " Arthur's seat."

None of Arthur's knights are mentioned by Drayton, and no romantic deeds are recounted. This may be due in part to Drayton's use of Geoffrey rather than Malory as a source, but his choice of source is determined by his serious historical purpose in writing. Merlin is the only figure usually associated with Arthur that is brought into the story. Drayton tells of Merlin's birth at " Caer-merdhin " and of his association with Stonehenge and with Vortigern's castle, where the conflict between the red and the white dragon brought out the prophecy that the Saxons would overcome the British, of his wish to build a wall of brass around Caermarthen, and of his imprisonment in a cave by " his Fay." He praises Merlin's prophecies and in the Tenth Song gives a brief resumé of them. Selden takes definite issue with Drayton on the subject of Merlin. To the story of the incubus conception he gives no credence, stating that this legend is as uncertain as many other fabulous tales connected with him, " seeing no perswading authority in any of them, rectifies the vncertainty." In the address " To the Reader from the Author of the Illustrations " Selden states concerning the " Prophecies out of Merlin," that he does not wish the reader to " impute " to him " any serious respect of them." Selden expands Drayton's account of the prophecies for the sake of clearness, but does not credit Merlin with " true foreknowledge." In the part played by Merlin in the begetting of Arthur he sees the influence of Greek mythology in the creation of a British myth. In regard to Stonehenge a summary of the theories of origin is presented, and the reader left to form his own judgment. He distinguishes between Merlin Sylvester and Merlin Ambrosius, pointing out that the latter, who was the reputed prophet, was not living in Arthur's time.

Drayton's real interests were wholly British. He wrote the play *Owen Tudor* in 1600; he included references to Arthurian matter in *England's Heroicall Epistles;* he dedicated the *Ballad of Agincourt* to the Cambro-Britans; he dedicated the *Polyolbion* to the Prince of Wales and prefaced it with an epistle " to my Friends the Cambro-Britans "; he held it to be more honorable to be derived from the British than from the Saxon line, and so stressed the British ancestry of James. He boasted that though the Saxons could shut up the British within a narrow realm, they could not " our mightie minds deiect." He thought of Wales as " the Nurse of all the *British* race " and the section which gave Tudor and ultimately the present king. Drayton's British sympathy even led him to twist facts. He states that the Welsh could not be conquered until Llewelin's death when " all-ruling Heaven would have us to resigne," though Selden shows that " the truth of Storie " reveals how the Welsh, meanwhile, had put themselves under English protection and had become the subjects of England.

In spite of his marked British sympathy Drayton, in writing over a period of time which covered the growing Jacobite disfavor, seems to reflect something of the changing attitude of the nation. He had personal reasons for disliking the king. He wrote two poems upon the accession of James, hoping to win preferment. James, however, sensed the impropriety of Drayton's failure to lament the queen and rebuffed Drayton. Drayton speaks of this incident in his *Epistle to George Sandys,* 1627:

> It was my fault before all other men
> To suffer shipwreck by my *forward pen*
> When King James entered.

The Owl reflects something of Drayton's bitterness in its satire upon the court. In the Thirteenth Song of the *Polyolbion* Drayton praises the solitary life of the hermit in contrast with the corrupt life of the courtier. In his elegy to William Browne, *Of the Evil Time,* he speaks against the ranks of the nobility filled by the creation of knights by James, and in the poem to Sir John Beaumont he deplores the degeneracy of the times. Perhaps this personal grudge in addition to the growing interest of the people in the Saxons helped to make his treatment of the Saxons as complimentary as it is. The Saxons are especially praised for their Christian kings and for their laws. Kent in the Eighteenth Song is cited for not allowing " forraine Lawes " to bind her ancient customs and for showing thereby that she was " of the ancient *Saxon* kind." In the Twelfth Song

Wrekin defends the Saxons as the Cambrian Hills had defended the British. The Saxons in fighting against the Danes had shown themselves as valiant as the British, and in Guy of Warwick they boasted a hero whose story was comparable to Arthur's in glorifying the race. Drayton shows the line of Saxon and Norman descent and how the two races are really one, being reunited with the coming of the Conqueror, a fact upon which the lawyers were basing their claims of Parliamentary rights. One cannot feel, however, that Drayton in this section shows the same warmth of personal bias as in the British portions of his poem. His treatment is formal, after a set pattern, and lacks the spirit and verve of the earlier sections. It is extremely noticeable that Drayton gives only four lines to the Greatest Saxon king and that Selden, noting the brevity of the treatment of Alfred, is constrained to add verses from Huntingdon.

Selden in his notes to the *Polyolbion* seems little influenced by Drayton's British leanings. Through his Saxon studies he had become convinced of the superiority of the Saxons to the British and of the true origin of the race. His growing legal knowledge set him definitely against the king, and this attitude further influenced his reaction toward British legend. Toward Arthur he is positively skeptical, saying, " His birth, actions, and all those too fabulously mixt stories," as well as the account of his burial, are not to be trusted. At times, therefore, he discredits a fabulous story by appending a jocular note. Again he takes serious issue with his source, as in the case of Leland's report of Arthur's seal. At other times he explains Drayton's allusion but reveals his own conviction that the details given are only a myth, sometimes even pleading with the reader not to take the matter seriously, saying, " I insert oft, out of the *British* story, what I importune you not to credit." For accounts of the stories of Arthur and the romances of his knights " with their prodigious performances " he sends the reader to Caxton, who has digested the material from " divers *French* and *Italian* fables." " From such," says Selden, "I abstaine, as I may." His conclusion is that the age of Arthur is so far removed that it is doubtful if anyone can ever separate the true from the false. Like many other " Worthies " Arthur has suffered from stories that are " too hyperbolique "; and though one may accept his kingship as authentic, the accounts of the conquest of a world empire are so extravagant that they shake one's belief:

The *Bards* songs haue, with this kind of vnlimited attribut so loaden him, that you can hardly guesse what is true of him.

In the *Analecta Anglo-Britannica* Selden's interest in the period after Caesar is in the introduction of Christianity and in the formation of the laws, and so the stories of Arthur find no place even as legendary matter in this serious discussion.

William Slatyer in his *Palae-Albion,* a versified chronicle history of England dedicated to James, is writing under the acknowledged influence of Drayton

just at the time when matters are coming to a crisis
between the king and Parliament and the British
material may be useful in bolstering up the wavering
loyalty of the people. Like Drayton he recounts all the
British legends as serious historic truth. There is too
much questioning, he says; it is a " Sicke Age ":

> When nothing once, so firme was thought,
> That now's not vnder Quare's brought:
> Though more staid heads will one day see,
> Such too much medling should not bee.
> Or by experience learne, at last,
> That hee's not wisest, prates too fast.

The critics must show better reasons for their distrust
or else cease their criticisms. The Roman period, which
other historians of the century welcomed as being
recounted with unquestionable authority, is attacked by
Slatyer even more strongly than by Drayton on the basis
that the Romans could not give a just account of their
predecessors on the island. Caesar " had small skill to
reade the *Brittish* Annalls o'ere ": he had " less leisure "; the British records were not to be trusted with a
conqueror and had been hidden in " Mona's secret
Cells," from whence the bards have " Rais'd *Brute* and
Arthur from their grave." The story of Uther's war
with Octa, his love for Igerne, and the birth of Arthur
is given in Canzone viii of Ode VII, and the story of
" Great Arthur's prowesse " follows in Canzone ix.

Bacon in the *History of Henry VII* concludes that in
Arthur's acts " there is truth enough to make him

famous, besides that which is fabulous." Taylor includes
the picture of Arthur and an account of his reign and
conquest of a continental empire. The emphasis given
to all the British monarchs shows where Taylor's sympathy lies. When he comes to the Saxons, he merely
lists the kings for each division of the Heptarchy.
Baker, credulous and superstitious in many matters, is
critical in his attitude towards Geoffrey, regretting that
all the labor of Geoffrey's numerous detractors cannot
" keep many at this day, from giving credit to his Fictions." The great number of " Commentitious Fables "
that he included " rendred even what truths he writ
suspected," so that Arthur " might well be reckoned
amongst the Fabulous." Yet in spite of these facts
Baker does not wholly reject the legend of Arthur: he
summarizes his acts, tells of the founding of the Round
Table, and gives Merlin's prophecy, which he considers
fulfilled in James.

During the troubled days of the Civil War and
the renewed conflict between the king and Parliament,
and during the Commonwealth, the interest of the
nation was again absorbed in the Saxons. Upon the
ancient laws of the nation depended the right of the
people to revolt against and depose a king. The interest in this law was so great that Lambarde's *Archeonomia* was published again in 1644. In his official defense
of the action of the English people in deposing and
beheading their king, Milton bases his argument upon
the idea of the contract made between the king and his

subjects in the coronation oath. In *Tenure of Kings and Magistrates* he cites from " our ancient books of law " to show that " the peers and barons of England had a legal right to judge the king." The whole argument of *Eikonoclastes* was concerning the supremacy of Parliament and the nature of the coronation oath. This is the coronation oath of Alfred, " the most worthy king, and by some accounted first absolute monarch of the Saxons here," and it limits the power of the king to the execution of the laws made by the people. Milton strengthens his statements concerning this oath by giving its meaning from both the Latin and Old English. He also points out that Charles has magnified his prerogative and that the idea of Divine Right is false:

A parliament is by all equity and right above a king, and may judge him, whose reasons and pretensions to hold of God only, as his immediate vicegerent, we know how far-fetched they are, and insufficient.

If the king violates his power, the penalty is stated in " the crown oath of Alfred," which says that the " king should be as liable, and obedient to suffer right, as others of his people."

Milton's first-hand knowledge of the ancient law is shown by the entries in his Commonplace book from Selden's *De Jure,* Spelman's *Concilia,* and Lambarde's *Archeonomia,* and by his references in *Eikonoclastes* to Bracton, to Fleta, and to " an ancient law-book called *The Mirror."* Milton undoubtedly shared with his age the respect for the Saxons as the great founders of the law, and stated in the *Areopagitica* that such investigations as Selden's were of great service "toward the speedy attainment of what is truest." In *Of Reformation* he had called the laws of Parliament "the holy covenant of union and marriage between the king and his realm," and had spoken of the "law giving and sacred Parliament" as "our highest court." In the national crisis, then, when Milton was seeking to express for the country its sense of right in judging its king, he relied upon the Saxon conception of sovereignty for the justification of the deed: the supreme authority was in Parliament; if the king violated his coronation oath, then Parliament might "take all power, authority, and the sword out of his hand."

During this period accounts of Arthur disappear. When the first volume of Dugdale's *Monasticon Anglicanum* appeared in 1655, the only interest revealed in Arthur was purely antiquarian. In connection with the account of Glastonbury Monastery, Dugdale gives some space to a discussion of Arthur's last days at Glastonbury and his gifts to the institution, but nothing is said of his great deeds or of his knights.

Thomas Heywood in 1641 made an attempt to revive belief in Merlin with as little success as met the effort to restore Arthur to favor. The complete title to his work gives a condensed summary of the content and a good idea of the method of treatment: *The Life of Merlin, surnamed Ambrosius; his Prophecies and Predictions Interpreted, and their Truth made Good by our*

English Annals: being a Chronographical History of all the Kings and Memorable Passages of the Kingdom, from Brute to the Reign of King Charles. Heywood portrays Merlin as an honored seer, recounts the dragon prophecy, associates him with Uther and Arthur, and then shows how his prophecy has been fulfilled " genuinely and properly" until the time Charles I came to the throne. He even argues with the reader for belief in Merlin on the grounds that Merlin was " a professed Christian and therefore, his auguries the better to be approved and allowed." A different person this from the son of the peasant woman and the cloven-hoofed incubus portrayed by Rowley or from the mere prognosticator which he shortly became!

The story of the degeneration of Merlin is an interesting one. During the uneasy days of the Civil War Merlin's fame was used to lend credence to all sorts of predictions and prophecies, and the strictly political nature of Merlin's prophecies disappeared. William Lilly, the leading astrologer of the seventeenth century, produced an almanac in April, 1644, entitled " Merlinus Anglicus Junior, the English Merlin Reviv'd, or a Mathematicall Prediction upon the affairs of the English Commonwealth." This is interesting for our study chiefly because the title is reminiscent of the enchantment of Merlin and his immurement in a cave. The almanac had an immediate popularity, and the first edition was exhausted in a week. A second edition was published the same year. Lilly used the name of Merlin

in the title of several prophetic pamphlets. Even Elias
Ashmole translated the " Prophecies of Ambrose Merlin, with a key," and Lilly included it in some of the
copies of " The World's Catastrophe, or Europe's many
mutations untill 1666." The prophecies were also
extended to include any unusual occurrence, as is shown
by the title, " A Prophesie (of Merlin) concerning Hull
in Yorkshire, 1642." More trivial matter, however,
was to find shelter under Merlin's name, and he does
not regain a place of dignity until the romantic revival.
Mead's *Merlin,* the *British Museum Catalogue,* and the
Cambrian Bibliography tell the story. There were a
few editions of the old prophecies, including Heywood's *Life of Merlin* (1651), and there was one example of the serious use of British prophecy in a poem,
Chamberlayne's *Pharonnida,* but in general, Merlin's
name was used to cover almanacs, astrological observations, and any other type of prognostication. An example of a popular type is " The Mad-merry Merlin; or
the Black Almanack: comprising strange observations,
and monthly prognostications . . . in the ensuing year
. . . 1654." The Merlin predictions are burlesqued in
Thomas Randolph's poem, " An Apology for his false
Prediction that his Aunt Lane would be delivered of a
Son." Taylor had done a similar thing when he attributed to Merlin the prediction of the birth of Archy
Archibald Armstrong. Merlin's accepted position during the second half of the seventeenth century is very
well stated by Lorece in Sir Aston Cockain's *The Obsti-*

nate Lady when Lorece tells Vandona who Merlin was:

He was an intricate prognosticator of firmamental eclipses, and vaticinated future occurrents by the mysterious influences of the sublime stars and vagabondicall planets.

The depths of degradation reached by Merlin are related by Defoe, who in the *Journal of the Plague Year* tells that Merlin's head was used as a sign by the fortune tellers. Merlin's association with Stonehenge was exploded, also, during this period. Shortly after the middle of the century arose that controversy over Stonehenge in which Inigo Jones contended for a Roman origin and Walter Charleton, Dugdale, and others attributed a Danish origin. In this architectural and archeological discussion the name of the magician was lost from the greatest of all the legends associated with his name.

A revival of the political usage of Merlin's prophecy took place just before the Restoration when Thomas Pugh in his *Brittish and Out-landish Prophesies* (1658) gave emphasis to the British descent of Charles and pointed out that in the return of Charles to England was to be seen the return of King Arthur which had been so long expected. He included " His Highness's lineal descent from the antient Princes of Brittain, clearly manifesting that Hee is the Conqueror they so long prophesied of." Pierce Enderby in 1661 also traced the ancestry of Charles back to the British, and as is indicated by the title, *Cambria Triumphans, or*

Brittain in its Perfect Lustre, saw in the Restoration the culmination of England's glory.

Perhaps Charles himself had become interested in accounts of Arthur when he was exiled in France, for the young prince, Louis XIV, was being instructed in " les actions heroïques, et les occupations d'honneur des plus braves Cheualiers des siecles passez " by means of Vulson de la Colombière's *Le Vray Théâtre d'Honnevr et de Chevalerie.* In the dedication to Mazarin the author says that since the nobility can no longer be distinguished from the base-born, it is necessary " remettre la noblesse dans son ancien lustre, et dans ses priuileges et prerogatiues." Accordingly, he gives an account of the knights of the Round Table to illustrate the highest order of nobility and the customs anciently observed. He includes a sketch of Arthur's character and deeds, a brief account of each knight and his particular enemy, and a description of the coat of arms of each knight. Guinevere and her enemy, Morgain le Fée, are the only women included. In Chapter IV a description of the Arthurian tournament is presented as a model for tournaments. Frequently the author illustrates some point of chilvalric procedure from the stories of the Round Table, using all this material as though it were absolutely authentic.

Some further British interest is shown by the fact that in 1663 Silas Taylor in his *History of Gavelkind* goes out of his way to include a defense of Geoffrey and the British legends. Sheringham in 1670 also takes

up the defense of the entire ancient story and writes
De Anglorum Gentis Origine Disceptatio to review the
whole dispute over the Trojan origin. He defends
Geoffrey as a reputable historian, and fully accepts
Geoffrey's complete account of Arthur.

In the same year, however, Milton, who had completed his *British History* in 1655 but had never given
it to the publisher, came out with a violent counter-
attack on Geoffrey and a positive expression of disbelief
in both the Trojan origin and the legend of Arthur.
He will not even use Geoffrey as a source except " when
others are all silent," and when he is forced to use
Geoffrey, he casts aspersions upon him. At one time he
will point out in Geoffrey's material " the simple fraud
of this Fable "; at another he will sneer at his authority
as one " whose weight we know." Milton says of Geoffrey:

What he was, and whence his authority, who in his age or
before him have deliver'd the same matter, and such like
general discourses, will better stand in a Treatise by themselves.

Though such a treatise was never written, Milton cannot refrain from taking up these points as he writes his
history. He calls Geoffrey's source " that fabulous
book" and shows how strange it is that this book
should be " utterly unknown to the World, till more
than 600 years after the dayes of Arthur." Milton discredits the British, disproves the valor of Arthur, and
even questions the existence of any such person, while
he presents the Saxons in a most favorable light, as we

shall see in more detail in another chapter. Such an attitude is what we should expect from the author of *Eikonoclastes.*

Aylett Sammes follows Milton in his proof that Arthur could not have been so great as reputed and quotes the attack of Scriverius, the author of the *Antiquities of Batavia,* upon Geoffrey to the effect that Geoffrey's history is " Groote grove lange dicke taste lijck ende unbeschaemte logen "—that is "A most impudent Lie, a great one, a heavy one, a long thick one, which (like the Aegyptian Darkness) was so palpable it might be felt." Like Speed, Sammes sees in a body of fable the seed of truth and accepts Arthur as an " eminent person . . . a Man of excellent parts, far beyond any of his Age." Churchill in 1675 expresses the opinion that the credit of Arthur had been lessened " by those that labour to magnifie it." Stillingfleet follows the same line as Milton and Sammes to show Arthur as less powerful than reputed. He sketches the controversy regarding Geoffrey, lining up the followers of Geoffrey and those who ridicule his story, making a fine analysis of all the earlier historical accounts. Matters of antiquity, he holds, " depend upon the comparing of ancient Histories, the credibility of Testimonies, and a sagacity in searching, and skill in judging concerning them." Having followed this method of study himself, he arrives at a very sane and modern conclusion concerning Arthur:

I think both sorts are to blame about him, I mean those who

tell *Incredible Tales* of him, such as are utterly inconsistent with the *Circumstances* of the *British Affairs* at that time; and those who deny there was any such Person, or of any considerable *power* among the *Britains.*

In the same year Crouch included a brief history of Arthur in his *England's Monarchs from the Romans to this Time,* and in 1694 followed it with the *English Monarchs with Poems and Pictures of every Monarch.* The next year his *History of the Principality of Wales* was published. This contains " A brief Account of the Antient Kings and Princes of Brittain and Wales till the final Extinguishing of the Royal Brittish Line," in which he gives without question the Arthurian story. Sir William Temple is of an entirely different attitude from that of Crouch. In speaking of Arthur's reign and achievements, he says doubtfully, " if any such there were," and adds that it " remains in doubt, whether to consider them as a Part of the Story of that, or the Fables of succeeding Ages." Certainly accounts of the Round Table and the stories of chivalry are not to be credited at all; such tales were introduced in imitation of the Spanish Romances. Wynne, who accepts the entire Geoffrey story, also gives an account of Arthur, but William Nicolson in the *Historical Library,* though he quotes the defenders of Geoffrey, gives as his own view an opinion similar to Stillingfleet's:

I am not for *wholly rejecting* all that's contain'd in that History, believing there is somewhat of Truth in it, under a mighty Heap of Monkish Forgeries.

James Tyrrell at the end of the century says that one cannot " positively affirm " that all is " absolutely false " and devotes four pages to the story of Arthur. He answers Milton on the identity of Arthur and feels that we should accept the main outlines of the stories centered about Arthur as king.

With the growing dissatisfaction with James II, there arose a definite opposition to the view that the ancient laws of the nation, either British or Saxon, were legal and an effort to prove that the true origin of the law was to be found in William the Conqueror. The loyalists wished to prevent any likelihood of a recurrence of deposition, supported (as in the case of Charles I) on the grounds of fundamental rights. Among the *Tracts* published by Peter Heylyn in 1681 is one " proving the kingly power neither co-ordinate with nor subordinate to any other on earth"; this bears the appropriate title, *Stumbling-block of Disobedience and Rebellion.* Passages in Nicholas Bacon's *Laws and Government of England* which attributed ultimate authority to the people instead of to the king and declared that the king was not the chief ruler, resulted in the persecution of the publisher in 1682. At Oxford University on July 21, 1683, a decree was passed " in their Convocation " against all such books as those deriving civil authority from the people, upholding the idea of a contract between the king and people, or supporting the right of deposition. Such doctrines and books, including the work of Milton, were termed " false, seditious

and impious; and most of them to be also Heretical and
Blasphemous, infamous to Christian Religion, and
destructive of all Government in Church and State."
Robert Brady's *Introduction to Old English History*
(1684) is to preach against " two sorts of Turbulent
Men ": those who hold that the origin of government
is in the people and that kings as " Executors and Trus-
tees . . . may be Tryed, Sentenced, Deposed, or put to
death by them "; and those who " hold forth to the
people, *Ancient Rights* and *Privileges,* which they have
found out in *Records* and *Histories,* in *Charters,* and
other *Monuments* of *Antiquity."* Brady refutes what
Coke and Selden have said about the conquest and
answers three tracts: William Petit's *Rights of the
Commons asserted, Argumentum Antinormanicum,* and
Exact History of the Succession of the Crown. His
Complete History of England, dedicated to James II,
continues this line of argument, attacking Selden and
Coke for what they have to say on " fundamental
rights," and stating that there can be no such thing as
a *pact* between the king and the people. Any rights and
liberties which the people may enjoy are derived from
the king to whom due gratitude should be rendered.
The purpose of these works is largely legalistic, and so
the reports of the British and Saxon conflict are composed of the barest facts. Though Brady indicates
acquaintance with Geoffrey, he makes no use of his
material and does not even mention Arthur.

When the Revolution took place, a number of writers

went to some pains to show that James abdicated and was not deposed by William of Orange, for there had grown up considerable feeling in support of the idea that the nation was not within its rights in deposing a king. An anonymous writer of 1689, however, presents anew the continuity of fundamental rights and answers such contentions as Brady's in a work entitled *A Seasonable Treatise: Wherein it is proved that King William (commonly call'd the Conqueror) did not get the Imperial Crown of England by the Sword, but by the Election and Consent of the People.* To clarify the issues James Tyrrell summarized in thirteen dialogues all the " chief arguments " both for and against " the late Revolution." These arguments are concerned with such questions as Divine Right, whether the king or Parliament is the " Sole Supreame Legislative Power," whether a king may " fall from, or forfeit his Royal Dignity for any breach of an Original Contract, or wilful violation of the Fundamental Laws of the Kingdom." In 1695, the year of the conspiracy against William, Temple clearly states in his *Introduction* to the History of England that William the Conqueror bound himself to sustain the ancient laws and " the ancient Customs and Liberties of the People, that were called the Common Law of the Kingdom."

With the return to ancient times for the support of the Revolution there occurred a renewal of the use of old story for political purposes, but instead of Saxon story, as one might surmise from the interest in law and the liberties of the people, it was again British story to which Blackmore, an ardent supporter of the king, turned for a parallel under which to present William's victorious entry into England. The reason for the presentation of William as Arthur is not, I think, hard to discover. To Blackmore the Roman Catholics were pagans, and identifying the pagans and Saxons, Blackmore respresented the Protestant William as the great Christian Champion, King Arthur. Further discussion of this curious literary revival of the Arthurian story in the reign of William III will follow in the next two chapters.

We have seen that the interest in Arthurian story in the seventeenth century fluctuated with the political developments in the nation. The reign of James I, beginning with the traditional heralding of the return of the golden age upon the succession of one of British line to the throne, became a period of vital interest in all things Saxon, through the desperate need of defending by Saxon law the rights of Parliament against the claim of Divine Right. The study of the Saxon language enforced by the practical need of reading the Saxon documents developed rapidly, and the language became of interest *per se.* The etymology of words, as well as the similarity of thought and custom, revealed that the nation should look for her true source among the Gauls rather than among the Trojans, and caused a debate in regard to the Trojan and Saxon original that resulted in the gradual abandonment of the mythical story of Brutus and real doubt as to the historicity of Arthur. Serious interest in Arthurian legend, so closely allied with the fortunes of the Tudors and consequently of the Stuarts, practically disappeared with the ascendancy of Parliament, and ridicule of the legend arose. A brief revival of interest was naturally associated with the Restoration, but perhaps the most remarkable development of the entire century was the application at the close of the century of Arthurian legend to William of Orange and the reopening of the defense of the British Worthy.

CHAPTER THREE

TROJAN AND SAXON IN LITERATURE

The change from British to Saxon interest which we have traced in the preceding chapters is not confined to the historical and political writings of the seventeenth century or even to the historical and epic verse. It is reflected in other types of literature as well. As was shown in the first chapter, the century began with the focal point of interest in Arthur. With the gradual centering of interest in the Saxons, their laws, documents, customs, and language, the British prepossession decreased; indeed, it had almost lapsed when the association of Charles II with the British brought about a temporary renewal of interest. This was short lived, however, and a barren period followed, lasting until the final decade of the century when Arthurian matter had a brief revival in Dryden and Blackmore.

The poets in the century revealed the popular regard for Arthur by the frequency of their references to him. It is to this feeling that Shakespeare appealed. Falstaff, who is associated with both court and tavern, enters in *Henry IV, Part ii* singing Deloney's ballad, " When Arthur first in Court." It is Arthur whom Mrs. Quickly substitutes for Abraham when she reports that Falstaff has gone to " Arthur's bosom," and of the two we feel that she has made the better choice. Henry V boasts that he is Welsh, and the valiant Fluellen assures the

king that he is proud of his countryman. It seems likely
that Shakespeare's sympathetic portrayal of the Welsh
may not only be attributed to his early and pleasant
associations with certain Welsh characters at Stratford
but also to the widespread tendency to seek a British
original for the nation. It is matter for boasting with
Justice Shallow that he has acted the rôle of Sir Dagonet
" in Arthur's show." Desiring to administer complete
disgrace to Oswald, Kent thinks in terms of the defeated
Arthurian knights who had to report their shame to
Arthur at Camelot, and wishes that he had Oswald upon
Sarum plain that he might drive him " cackling home to
Camelot." The parody of Merlin's prophecy by the Fool
in *King Lear* is doubtless correctly considered a somewhat later interpolation by the actor of the rôle, since
the tendency to ridicule the prophecies of Merlin arose
with the growing disfavor of James. It is more significant for Shakespeare's own interests to find him choosing British material for two of his mature plays, *King
Lear* and *Cymbeline*. Furthermore, the portrayal of the
Trojans in a more favorable light than the Greeks in
Troilus and Cressida was probably influenced by the fact
that the British traced their descent from the Trojans.
Dryden makes this interpretation when in his *Troilus
and Cressida* Shakespeare's Ghost as Prologue says:

> My faithful scene from true records shall tell,
> How Trojan valour did the Greek excel:
> Your great forefathers shall their fame regain,
> And Homer's angry ghost repine in vain.

Scott appends a note to explain that the British acceptance of the Trojan origin had " induced their poets to
load the Grecian chiefs with every accusation of coward-
ice and treachery, and to extol the character of the Trojans in the same proportion."

We have noted Ben Jonson's interest in Arthurian
material and use of the legend in connection with court
entertainments. As we shall see in the discussion of
Arthur as epic subject, he also considered using this
material in an epic. His interest in the British continued
after he had abandoned the idea of an epic, and in 1629,
we learn, he was trying to secure Dr. Davies's *Welsh
Grammar* through James Howell. Howell speaks of the
fact that Jonson already has many Welsh grammars,
but does not cease his efforts to find this particular one,
which he uses as a New Year's gift, 1630, sending it
with a poem in praise of that language in which Merlin
made his prophecies and Arthur, " the first 'mongst
Christian Worthies," spoke.

A play portraying Vortigern's defeat by Aurelius and
Uther Pendragon was written before 1605, but not published. This shows the British as superior in power and
character to the Saxons and is of especial interest in its
picture of Uther. It has been published from the Lans-
downe manuscripts in *Shakespeare Jahrbuch,* XXXIV.
The descendants of Brute were also given full measure
of praise in a play entitled *Fuimus Troes* " publikely
represented by the Gentlemen Students of Magdalen
Colledge, in Oxford." This play was published in 1633,

but it is not definitely known when it was first acted.
Chetwood dates it as early as 1603; but if Wood's attribution of the play to Jasper Fisher is correct, the date
must be placed later, for Fisher did not enter Magdalen
Hall until 1607. A song in Scottish dialect at the end
of Act III has been taken to indicate an attempt to
please James, but there is no evidence on this point.
Since all the other acts end with songs by the Druids,
such an assumption seems plausible enough and, if true,
would date the play before 1625. Geoffrey's account of
Cassibelan's valiant stand against Caesar is the source
of the play, and emphasis is given to the Trojan descent
of the British. The soldiers are addressed as " the heirs
of mighty Brute," and Cassibelan says to Caesar:

> As you from Troy, so we, our pedigree do claim;
> Why should the branches fight, when as the root's the same?

Caesar replies that he grieves to draw sword " against
the stock of thrice-renowned Troy," and he has cause
for grief before the conflict is over, for his sword is
taken from him and he flies in disgrace, his army completely routed. The Romans stay away a year, and upon
their return to Britain are at first again routed. It is
only by the aid of the deserting British that Caesar is
able to overcome these " undaunted minds from Troy,"
and at the close of the play it is the boast of Cassibelan
that it was the glory of Britain that " none but a Julius
Caesar could her tame." Throughout the play the
British are presented in the most favorable light, and
even the structure of the play shows emphasis upon the

strength of the British. It is not until the fourth scene of Act IV that affairs begin to turn in Caesar's favor, and not until the sixth scene of Act V that Cassibelan consents to compound with Caesar. Middleton and Rowley, both using Geoffrey as their source, dramatized the conflict between the British and the Saxons, portraying the British in the more favorable light and concluding their plays with the British victorious. Though Rowley in *The Birth of Merlin* burlesques the mystic birth of the seer in representing the mother and uncle as ridiculous peasants and the father as a cloven-hoofed demon, he depicts Merlin himself as a serious child engrossed in books and gives him a splendid dignity, especially in the interpretation of the fight between the red and the white dragons and in his prophecy of Arthur. The plot is centered about the conflict of Aurelius and Uther against the usurping Vortigern. Aurelius, poisoned by the treachery of the Saxons through his Saxon wife, leaves Uther to regain the kingdom by defeating Vortigern and the Saxons. Rowley appeals to contemporary interest in the restoration of the name of Britain to England when in a speech to Vortigern, who is called "base destroyer of thy Native Countrey," Uther relates how the Saxons are establishing themselves in England and seek

> To blot the Records of old Brute and Brittains
> From memory of men, calling themselves
> Hengist-men, and Brittain Hengist-land, that no more
> The Brittain name be known.

Finally, though Merlin reveals to the victorious Uther that the Saxons will ultimately gain the land, he encourages him by the prediction of Arthur's conquest of a world empire, his establishment of the Round Table, and his great fame with which " all aftertimes shall fill their Chronicles," and by a vision of the triumphant Arthur and his successor, Constantine. Middleton's *The Mayor of Queenborough* (c. 1621?) places the emphasis upon the struggle between Vortigern and Aurelius, though Uther also appears in the play. The play ends with the rightful victory of Aurelius over Vortigern and the allied Saxons, Hengist and Horsus. Aurelius then pledges himself

> . . . to see this realm secur'd
> From the convulsions it hath long endur'd.

Two other plays approximately contemporary with these deal with the early British, showing an interest in pre-Arthurian times. It is no surprise to find one of these by Rowley. *A Shoo-maker a Gentleman* (acted 1609) depicts the struggle between the British and the Romans, emphasizing the valor of the British though defeated, and attributing the victory of the Roman Emperor, Diocletian, in France to the prowess of the British soldiers whom he had drafted to assist him. *The Valiant Welshman, or the true Chronicle History of the Life and Valiant Deeds of Caradoc, the great King of Cambria, now called Wales* (1615) by R. A. gives an exaggerated account of the British hero Caractacus (Caradoc). Samuel Rowley also gives a brief reference to the times of Arthur and represents the resurrected Arthur and his knights as aiding Henry VIII in his struggle against Catholicism. In *When you see me, you know me, or the famous Chronicle History of king Henrie the Eight* (1605), William Sommers cheers the heart of the king by reporting:

King *Arthur,* and his Knights of the round Table that were buried in Armour, are alive againe, crying Saint *George* for *England*, and meane shortly to conquere Rome.

Arthurian place association, fresh in the minds of the people, afforded opportunity for the poets to add significant connotation to their verse. Alexander Craig, for example, writing *To His Calidonian Mistress* tells how he lay weeping " beside the ditch profound " where " Guineuer dispairing Dame was dround," and would have " made end with her of love, and life, and all," had not time kindly filled in the ditch so that suicide was impossible! He consoles himself, therefore, by numbering his " plaints and cryes " by Merlin's " stones on *Sarum* plaine," which legend said could not be numbered. *Britannias Pastorals* is similar to the *Polyolbion* in the treatment of British tradition. Mona and Cambria are proud of their Trojan associations; the shepherds of Cornwall point out " where *Arthur* met his death, and *Mordred* fell "; Thetis pauses at the Severn to hear the " Brittish Bards " sing of Brute

Striving in spight of all the mists of eld,
To have his *Story* more authenticke held.

Travel literature also reveals the popularity of Arthurian tradition. Richard Carew in his *Survey of Cornwall* reminds one of Camden, Drayton, or Browne in his accounts of the legends of Arthur. When he tells of his visit to Tintagel, for example, he relates the story of Arthur's begetting; and when he writes of Camelford, he incorporates an account of the battle between Arthur and Mordred. Fynes Moryson, following Camden with extreme closeness in that part of his itinerary in which he tells of England and Scotland, naturally includes all the major Arthurian references.

As in the preceding century there are no tales of Arthur's knights and their romantic adventures. John Davies of Hereford, himself Welsh, one who praised the Tudor and Trojan ancestry of the Stuarts in his dedication of *Microcosmus* to Prince Henry, has Paper complain of its waste in the unopened " volumes hugely written " of

> The Sonnes of *Aymon, Bevis, Gawen, Guy,*
> *Arthur,* the Worthy, writ vnworthily;
> Mirrour of Knighthood, with a number such.

Even the Elizabethan organization of Arthur's knights had disbanded, and in its place had sprung up the loosely-knit fellowship of the roaring boys. This change is noted in *The Maske of Flowers* " by the Gentlemen of Graie's Inne, Twelfth Night, 1613-14 ";

> The Worthies they were nine, 'tis true,
> And lately Arthur's Knights I knew;
> But now are come up Worthies new,
> The roaring boyes, Kawashae's crew.

A solitary romance connected with the Arthurian story appeared in the early years of the reign of King James: this is Richard Johnson's *The Most Pleasant History of Tom a Lincolne, that renowned soldier, The Red Rose Knight, who for his valour and chivalry was sirnamed The Boast of England*. Tom a Lincolne is Arthur's son by amour; and since his complete life history is given, a considerable portion of the story is devoted to King Arthur, throwing much new light upon the Worthy! The first of the romance takes up the account of Arthur's visit to London, his sojourn with Androgius, " Earle of London," his love for Angellica, the Earl's daughter, and his arrangement for Angellica to retire to a nunnery, so that their secret meetings may be less suspected. King Arthur is again given a prominent place in the story when he receives Tom a Lincolne, who has been brought up as a shepherd's son, into the court, and after testing him in various tournaments, makes him one of the knights of the Round Table. The beginning of Part Two of the romance gives a very curious account of how after his twelve battles with the Saxons and conquest of " the third part of the earth," Arthur betakes himself in his old age to a quiet life for seven years. Upon his death bed he confesses his guilty love and acknowledges Tom as his son, thereby bringing about many troubles, the story of which makes up the second part of the romance. Of all the knights of the Round Table Sir Lancelot is the only one who figures largely in the tale. He with Sir Tristam and Sir Triamore goes to bring the Red Rose Knight to Arthur's court; he accompanies Tom a Lincolne upon his adventures; in his lame old age he journeys with Tom a Lincolne's two sons to London, rejuvenated by the joy of seeing them; and finally, after the forty days of celebration held there, he goes with them to Lincoln. This tale is embellished with all the gore and the glory of the medieval romance, and its popularity is attested by the fact that it ran to seven editions by 1635. Encouraged by this success, Johnson produced in 1621 another story of a character in King Arthur's court, *The History of Tom Thumb*. This, however, is merely a prose account of the material known through old ballads and is of little interest.

In contrast with this prevailing interest in the British there arose some popular attention to the Saxon story, centered about Alfred. The range of this interest is somewhat indicated by the fact that an illustrated broadside in two parts was popular with the common people, and a controversy over Alfred as the founder of Oxford University was waged by the learned. Camden, whom we have seen concerned primarily with Saxon matters in his *Remains* of 1605, had been sufficiently interested in King Alfred to interpolate in the 1600 edition of his *Britannia* a passage attributing the founding of Oxford to Alfred. A few years later he produced a new edition of Asser's *Life of Alfred*. William Drury thought the attraction of the subject of Alfred of sufficient scope to insure the success of a play and wrote a Latin tragicomedy, *Aluredus or Alfredus* (acted 1619). This is concerned primarily with Alfred's conquest of the Danes and Cuthbert's work in Christianizing the people. Alfred has sought refuge on an obscure island in the hut of a cottager. Here he is finally discovered by his faithful generals. After secretly exploring the camp of the enemy for information, he is able to regain the kingdom from the Danes. The play ends by showing his adversary as converted and becoming his ally.

1625–1660

With the death of James and the succession of Charles the literary interest in the early inhabitants lapsed for a time. After the emphasis upon British legend found in the pageants and entertainments for Queen Elizabeth and King James, it is interesting to find Charles returning to stately processional, depending upon rich costumes, banners, and music to give splendor to his passage through London on the way to the coronation. Since there was no question of succession, there was no need for bolstering claims to the crown by legendary matter, and Charles was wise in emphasizing the dignity of the assumption of the throne by its rightful heir.

Charles was also the legitimate heir to the conflict originated by his father between the Crown and Parliament, and it was not long before this struggle was taken up with renewed vigor. With the development of this friction there appeared again in literature the conflict between interest in the British and interest in the Saxons.

In 1634 appeared the only edition of Malory produced during the century, having for its avowed purpose
a renewal of interest in Arthur. The publisher's preface
begins with a summarized history of Arthurian times,
" set downe to confute the errours of such as are of an
opinion that there was never any such man as king
Arthur." The author of the introduction argues for
Arthur on the ground that the other Worthies are
accepted without question:

And shall the Jewes and the Heathen be honoured in the
memory and magnificent prowesse of their worthies? shall
the French and Germane nations glorifie their triumphs with
their Godfrey and Charles, and shall we of this island be so
possest with incredulitie, diffidence, stupiditie, and ingratitude,
to deny, make doubt, or expresse in speech and history, the
immortall name and fame of our victorious Arthur. . . . As
(by the favour of Heaven) this kingdome of Britaine was
graced with one worthy, let us with thankfulness acknowledge
him; . . . let us not be more cruell then death to smother or
murder his name; or let us not be worse then the grave in
burying his favour.

The publisher not only paved the way for the favorable
reception of the book by his warm defense of Arthur,
but also equipped it with a title reminiscent of Spenser.
It is the only edition of Malory which bears the title
The History of Prince Arthur instead of *The History of
King Arthur.*

There is no evidence, however, that this edition of
Malory had any degree of popularity, for there was not
another edition until 1816. There is no record of the

publication of any of the Arthurian romances, following this edition of Malory, as one would expect if there had been a revival of interest. Apparently the romances were difficult to secure in England, even if one should want them. In January 1636-7 Sir Kenelm Digby wrote Lord Conway from Paris that he had been promised " La conqueste du sang real " and " the legend of Sir Tristram " for Lord Conway, and " can procure him an entire collection of the books known there of that kind." Sir Kenelm Digby's comment on Arthur shows belief in him and pride in his accomplishments:

England is happy in producing persons who do actions which after ages take for romances; witness King Arthur and Cadwallader of ancient time.

In 1633 the British appeared once more in a masque presented before the king and the queen. In *Coelum Britannicum* Thomas Carew represented Charles as the pole star with the queen as another star beside him; from these " British stars " the globe was to receive light. An anti-masque of Picts, " the natural inhabitants of this isle," and of " ancient Scots, and Irish " was given in order that the king and queen might see " The point from which your full perfections grew." For the maskers' dance Chorus called forth from a mountain representing England, Scotland, and Ireland, Arthur and his " choice band . . . richly attired like ancient heroes." These were preceded by " a troop of young lords and noblemen's sons . . . apparelled after the old British fashion." Chorus promised as dancing partner for the queen Prince Arthur or St. George, and for each lady " a Guy, a Bevis, or some true Round-Table knight."

In the masque presented at Whitehall " on the Sunday after twelfth night 1637 by the king's majestie and his lords," D'Avenant's *Britannia Triumphans,* Merlin is used as a " prophetic magician" to bring about miraculous changes in scene. First, Imposture asks that his many noted followers be revealed, and Merlin shows them in a " horrid hell." Merlin next presents a " mock Romanza " to show the damsel in distress, the dwarf and knight pitted against the giant, and the other characteristic features of the old romances in burlesque. Finally, Merlin is used to produce a chorus of contemporary poets. There is no association with Arthur; Merlin is merely an enchanter and magician.

Little additional British material is published until after the Restoration. Lodowick Carlell's *Arviragus and Philicia,* a story of British valor and success in warfare, was printed in 1639; and Francis Beaumont's lost play, *Madoc, King of Britain,* appeared before 1642. Cowley associated the struggle of the British and Saxons with the conflict between the king and Parliament and appealed for a display of the spirit of true Britains, a proof of Arthur's existence and prowess by their own valor:

> If any Drop of mighty *Vther* still
> Or *Vther's* mightier Son your Veins does fill,
> Show then that Spirit; 'till all Men think by you
> The doubtful Tales of your great *Arthur* true.

This is a very natural parallel since the Stuarts had emphasized their British descent, and Parliament was basing its claim to power upon the ancient rights of the Saxons. The ardent loyalist, Thomas Fuller, even went out of his way to include in his *Church History of Britain* a section in praise of the British language and an attack upon Bede for giving only enough British matter " to make a *Pedestall,* the more fairly to reare and advance his *Saxon* History thereupon." When Sir John Mennis and Dr. James Smith published their *Musarum Deliciae* in 1656, they included at the end of the collection an old ballad entitled *A Defiance to King Arthur and His Round Table.* This tells of the dwarf's message from Sir Rhines of Northgales demanding King Arthur's beard. Such defiance caused a din in the hall, and the dwarf was in danger for a time. Finally he was presented with one hundred pieces of gold and ordered to report to Sir Rhines that Arthur himself was coming to Northgales. When Arthur " shook his good Sword," the dwarf was left with no uncertainty as to his purpose. Ritson in *Bibliotheca Poetica* identifies the initials at the close of the ballad, " I. A.," as standing for James Aske, and says that the ballad is the identical one intended to have been sung at Kenilworth. Two romances of the period have some British interest. Sir Francis Kynaston uses a British hero and British scene for his " heroic Romance," *Leoline and Sydanis.* At the foot of Snowdon is a " stately castle," the home of " the old Brittain's King, Arvon the Great." Here a

Druid is confined in a cave by King Arvon and uses his supernatural power for revenge. King Arvon invests the walls of Caerleon, thinking that the father of the heroine has stolen his son. There is little British interest other than the place associations. Chamberlayne's *Pharonnida: an Heroic Poem in Five Books* is based largely upon British material, patterned after the Italian romances.

Travel literature, which had been the storehouse of legend, also reflects the lack of interest in Arthur. The traditions attached to the places associated with Arthur and Merlin are either unknown or else have no popular appeal. When William Brereton visited both Glastonbury and Winchester in 1635, he made no mention whatever of Arthur, and Nehemiah Wharton in 1642 seemed to think that Arthur was buried in St. Mary's Cathedral, Worcester. Taylor, the Water-Poet, who showed in his histories a definite British bias, made two tours of Wales in 1649 and 1652, respectively. Had the legends of Arthur been discussed, he would have been quick to reflect the interest and to play upon it for popularity. At Glastonbury he pieced some broken bits of marble and discovered the words:

Hic jacet Guiniverus Regina, Vxores, etc.

Apparently no one related to him the details of the legend associated with Glastonbury, for he merely inferred that since Guinevere was Arthur's wife, Arthur's bones " were not layd far from her." Camelford and Chester stirred no reminiscences; but Caermarthen revealed Merlin, though Taylor was far more engrossed by the fact that here " very fair Egs are cheaper than small Pears."

The failure of a conscious effort to bring about a revival of interest in British stories in the reign of Charles I is reflected in two ways: negatively it is shown by the indifference which we have just studied; positively it is revealed by ridicule of the British and by publication of Saxon matter. In striking contrast with the earlier idealization of Arthur and the British, we find Arthurian allusion taking a comic turn and Welsh characters given an unusual share of ridicule. Thomas Nabbes, for example, shows none of the traditional reverence for Arthur in *Tottenham Court* when he represents Stitchwell, who has discovered Changelove making love to Mrs. Stitchwell, as merrily remarking:

And have I tane you, sir *Lancelot?* Would you be billing with my *Guiniver?* . . . For this attempt King *Arthur* doth here degrade thee from a Knight of his round Table to bee a Squire of his Wife's body.

Middleton in *A Chaste Maid in Cheapside* portrays a Welshwoman as the mistress of Sir Walter Whorehound and a Welshman, Davy Dahanna, as his poor relative and attendant. The Welsh no longer receive the kindly, sympathetic comic touch of Shakespeare. There is no rounded portrayal of racial characteristics but rather a caricature. Through the Welsh is satirized the boast of derivation from Brute so prevalent in the earlier years of the Stuarts. Though he gets chronology a little confused, Randall, a comic Welshman in Rowley's *A Match at Midnight,* traces his genealogy from Brute through Cadwallader; he is " a Pritain of the plood of Cadwallader which Cadwallader was Prut's great grandfather." He is termed "choleric shred of Cadwallader " and fool, both of which terms he richly deserves. Caradoc in Randolph's *Hey for Honesty* is a true " leek of Wales " of " Pendragon's noble stock." The relationship even extends to clothes, for his " fery doublet is coshen-sherman to Utter Pendragon's sherken." When assigned to take charge of the wing of the army, he indignantly exclaims, " Brutus hish coshen look to the whing!" Even the lice with which he is troubled are descended from Aeneas through Silvius, Brutus, etc., and have ancestors which " fought in the wars of Troy, by this leek, as lustily as the lice of Troilus," nay, even of Hector! This is a different thing from the racial boast of genealogy such as is portrayed in the *Welch-man* of Heywood's *The Royall King and the Loyal Subiect,* or is parodied by Jonson and other dramatists. In Shirley's *Love Tricks* it is the trappings of the old romances that are ridiculed through a Welshman. Jenkins goes in pursuit of the girl he is wooing, who has fled in disguise to escape his attentions, but becomes very much afraid, for

Her have read in histories, and relations, kernicles, very famous knights, and prave sentilmen of valors, and shivalries, have been enchanted, look yar, in castles and very strong dwellings, and towers, and solitary places.

In contrast with this ridicule of the British upon the stage was the serious portrayal of the Saxons in two plays. Richard Brome's *The Queen's Exchange* gives the story of the Queen of the West Saxons and includes a vision of " Six Saxon Kings ghosts crown'd with Sceptres in their hands," which return to earth to look after the succession. In 1634 there appeared *A Saxon Historie, of the Admirable Adventures of Clodoaldus and his Three Children.* But by far the most interesting and curious use of Saxon material was the elaborate parallel drawn between Alfred and Charles I and appended to Robert Powell's *Life of Alfred.* It is significant that this work appeared in the year of the edition of Malory (1634) and presents Charles, who was sprung from " double British line," as " our now living Alfred " in whom " the fulnesse of his vertues " survive. Powell's own summary of his parallel gives a very good idea of the nature of the full discussion which has preceded it:

I have now presented to your favourable view, a paire of Peerlesse Princes, who for their religion, piety, devotion, institution and renovation of good lawes, government, justice, mercy, truth, meetnesse, temperance, patience, abstinence, conjugall castimony, and all other vertues, may be presidents of imitation to all Princes and people.

And this to Charles!

Three manuscripts, only one of which has even been published, are of considerable interest to the student of Arthurian legend. In Bishop Percy's *Folio Manu-*

script, written in a hand belonging approximately to the middle of the century, are set down some twelve selections dealing with Arthur and some of his knights. Since this manuscript remained unpublished until the nineteenth century, it can have had very limited influence upon seventeenth century thought and is important chiefly as the indication of the interest in medieval story felt by an individual.

Both of the unpublished manuscripts are political allegories of the reign of Charles I written by ardent loyalists. Because of the nature of the material they contained, they could not be published without danger; when the danger subsided, all point to the poems was lost, and they have, therefore, remained in manuscript to this day. The earlier of these, dated 1635 by a statement on the title page, is *A Supplement of the Faery Queene* probably by Robert Jegon. There are three long books written in Spenserian stanza, which purport to be books seven, eight, and nine of the *Faerie Queen.* Jegon in his preface cites Spenser's letter to Raleigh and says that in addition to the three books already written he intends to complete Spenser's plan by writing three more books to finish out the private moral virtues and continuing "untill in the person of Arthur, after he came to bee a King, I have framed the other part of politicke vertues." He terms the *Faerie Queen* "onely an exact treatise of Morall Philosophy enveloped in an Allegoricall Romance," and models his own moral allegory upon it. As in the *Faerie Queen* the hero of each of the three books is one of the knights of Gloriana's court and embodies a separate virtue, while Arthur is the sum of all these and other virtues and is used as a unifying link for the three books. Though we note the limiting word " onely " in the above description of the *Faerie Queen,* which would indicate that Jegon thought that there was no political significance in Spenser's poem, Jegon's obvious imitation of Spenser's method of handling political allegory in his own more easily understood references seems to throw light upon how one should approach the study of Spenserian political allegory. Jegon's poem is " consecrated . . . . to the immortall honour of my King, and Countrey," and is dedicated to Charles, who has restored the glory of the British and brought back the Golden Age:

> Thy soueraigne worth's the subiect of my Song:
> Thou sitts't in Arthur's seate and dost maintaine
> The antique glory of the Britons strong:
> Thou hast Astrea brought to earth againe,
> The Golden Age reviv'd is in thy raigne.

King Charles is the Arthur in this poem, and the virtues of Prudence, Fortitude, and Liberality depicted in the three books, respectively, are attributed in the opening stanzas of each book to Charles. Henrietta Maria is Gloriana, and England is " faery land." On the title page it is stated that in these books " are allegorically described Affaires both military and civill of these times "; and in order that the significant episodes may not be missed, the reader is given a clue to each book.

The first book is concerned with the religious struggle, typified by a fight between the armies of Caecozel and Doxethus, and more especially with the Irish disturbances; the other two books are taken up with affairs on the continent and in Scotland. As in Spenser it is the leading events of the reign and the prominent characters which one should seek to identify; the minor episodes and characters are the trappings of romance and not the significant points of the poem.

Arthur appears at intervals throughout the three books. It is he who knights Albanio, the hero of Book Seven, and who comes to the rescue of Albanio and fights the giant Granvanio later in the book. Arthur also rescues Callimachus, the hero of Book Eight, and accompanies him to the home of Panarete where he leaves him in safe hands. Callimachus relates to Panarete the stories of Arthegal, Guyon, "faire Britomart," and Calidore, and tells how the Red Cross Knight overcame the "blatant Beast." In canto eight of the same book Prince Arthur is shown fighting in a tournament to save a maiden who has sought aid in Gloriana's court against the overtures of a Spaniard. In Book Nine Belcour, the hero of the book, is asked to tell the story of Prince Arthur's court and relates how two knights fought, one of them with a spear wrought by Merlin. This spear had formerly been used unsuccessfully against Arthur, who was protected by a shield received from the Lady of the Lake. In canto eight Merlin is depicted reading a parchment. After his story is told,

Merlin becomes prophetic and relates that a royal hero will unite the land and bring peace, an obvious reference to James. Later in the canto Arthur is portrayed in another tournament, gloriously costumed, forcing fifty knights to flee before him, and winning the highest honors.

The other manuscript, which is preserved in the Bodleian, is an epic in six books written by Samuel Sheppard, an ardent supporter of Charles I, during various periods of imprisonment. It is entitled *The Faerie King,* and is written in obvious and avowed imitation of Spenser, whose spirit Sheppard constantly invokes and to whom he attributes his own inspiration. He does not, however, attempt to write in Spenserian stanzas, but adopts the more popular contemporary form of the heroic couplet. The poem is undated and the surmise of 1610 given in the *D. N. B.* is clearly incorrect; the *Postscript* to the poem has apparently been overlooked, for it furnishes ample evidence for an approximate date. In giving an account of the trying conditions under which the poem was composed, Sheppard states that the sixth book was written in " Peter House and Whittington Colledge alias Newgate," where he remained over fourteen months until the downfall, " by the hand of their owne Generalissimo the famous Cromwell," of the statesmen who had caused his imprisonment. Since his release it has been " almost foure yeares," during which time " maugre all opposition," he has brought his poem " to the perfection you see." These statements place the completion of the poem about the middle of the Commonwealth period. The opposition which the author encountered was due to the fact that the epic is a political allegory. Sheppard refuses, naturally, " to explaine and obviate the luminous misteries of most sacred Poesie " and contents himself with hinting that his poem is a " worke of more worth than either myselfe will boast, or permit others to divulge." As does the " *Supplement to the Faery Queene,* it embodies allegorically the chief events of the reign of Charles and is written for the glory of the king:

> Thy name (illustrious prince) shall here subsist
> Better then were the Memphian Trophies thine.

The political allegory is more virulent than that of Jegon and consequently more veiled. Again the allegory is rather general in its nature, dealing with the events of large significance in the reign of Charles. Since Sheppard makes such constant reference to his use of Spenser, it seems strange that he does not adopt Spenser's method of conveying moral allegory. The purpose of the epic is the same as that of the *Faerie Queen* as is revealed by the sub-title, " Fashioning Love and Honour." There is no attempt, however, to show the separate virtues in the separate books. Strangely enough, Arthur does not even appear as a character. There is, in fact, only one important reference to him. This is when Byanor, who has been the chief support of Prince Ariodant, is presented with a marvelous sword, " the same Prince Arthur, England's mighty

Lord, once wore." The sword now bears on its " golden Pummell " the inscription:

> (by Matyred St. Edwards hand set forth)
> the Two Faire Testaments that can, alone
> prescribe the true way to Salvation.

That so little reference is made to Arthur is probably due to the waning interest in British matter. Certainly the account of Merlin shows the effect of the decadence of the Merlin story, for Merlin, whose history is only briefly summarized, is depicted as an enchanter suffering torture in hell for his magic.

1660-1700

In the year of the Restoration there appeared the second Arthurian romance which the century produced, a romance unique in that it is devoid of all love element and is centered about the exploits of Arthur as king. This extraordinary work, of which I have seen no previous account, is *The Most Famous History of That Most Renowned Christian Worthy Arthur King of the Britaines, and his famous knights of the Round Table* by Martin Parker, the ballad maker. One is put into the mood for medieval romance by the magnificent mounted knight with his remarkable display of plumes which adorns the title page. The preface contains a defense of Arthur in which it is pointed out that the " Hyperbolical discourses " of Geoffrey and others have caused doubt in Arthur, but that he is no more to be doubted than William the Conqueror. Furthermore, he

is one of the three Christian Worthies and " to explode
one is to hisse all the rest from the stage of Christianity." There follows a marvelous story which takes
Geoffrey's *Historia* as its foundation and embellishes
it with further " hyperbolicall " details. In the first
chapter there is no hint of the stigma connected with
Arthur's birth. The Duke of Cornwall " prompted
by ambition, avarice, and oppulency . . . raised open
Rebellion against his Soveraigne," and is therefore
justly slain, after which " Igren " and Uther are married.
Later, in Chapter IV, Parker says in regard to Arthur's
legitimacy, " For although I do not, many then did
question his legitimacy "; but he dismisses the grounds
for this questioning as " not pertinent to our story."
The conquest of the Saxons by Arthur is magnificent.
In one battle fought on New Years Day (517) " 46000
Pagan Saxons were sent to the devil for a New years
gift." After twelve such defeats the Saxons who
remained alive left the kingdom," to which they never
returned during the raigne of Arthur, and his next successor." The challenge to single combat (which is from
Lotho, king of the Norwegians, instead of from Tollo)
includes a challenge from ten Norwegian knights to
ten followers of Arthur. In the combat not only did
Arthur kill Lotho, but the ten British knights slew " 6.
of their 10. Antagonists, and mortally wounded the
other four," not receiving any " notable hurt " themselves! Parker meant to present the defeat of the
Romans as a mere trifle accomplished upon Arthur's

journey home from subduing the Saracens in Palestine, but either overlooked it or left the chapter unfinished. Since the romance is a posthumous publication, one might consider the brevity of the chapter as an indication of the latter. Parker's crowning achievement is a list of one hundred and fifty knights of the Round Table from an " old Chaucerian manuscript," headed by a cut of ten knights in full armor seated around the table. This remarkable tale seems to have had immediate popularity, for there were two editions in the same year.

In 1622 *Ignoramus,* satirizing Common Law, was translated by Robert Codrington; the *Birth of Merlin,* which had remained in manuscript from the early days of James I, was published; and Fuller's *Worthies* appeared. The last presented Arthur as the " British Hercules " but dismissed the knights with the remark:

As for his Round Table, with his knights about it, the tale whereof hath trundled so smoothly along for many ages, it never met with much belief amongst the judicious.

The following year there was a second edition of the *Valiant Welshman,* but after this British matter again lost popularity.

Between the middle of the century and the Revolution the increasing Saxon interest which we have seen evidenced in history and scholarship was reflected in literature. Two dramatists found in the history of Edgar, king of the West Saxons, the material for exceedingly popular plays. Edward Ravenscroft in 1677 produced a play entitled *King Edgar and Alfreda,* which he prefaced by a " Life of Edgar as I find it in our English Chronicles." This play is probably more important as an indication of public interest in the subject than as an expression of the dramatist's concern for Saxon material, for Ravenscroft was merely a practical playwright looking for good stage drama, as is shown by the fact that in 1678 he adapted *Ignoramus.* Thomas Rymer's play has greater significance. It was licensed September 13, 1667, printed the following year, and ran to three editions, appearing again in 1691 and 1693. The dedication of the play is to the king and speaks of the king as comparable to Edgar in that he has built up the navy and preserved the peace. Rymer adds, " You alone, great Edgar's person bear."

In 1678 Obadiah Walker published Spelman's *Life of Alfred,* translated into Latin. His Latin dedication to the king contains a parallel of Alfred and Charles II similar to that drawn by Robert Powell between Alfred and Charles I. Both Charles II and Alfred had been victorious in wars and had magnanimously restored laws and possessions to the conquered. Both had done much for the improvement of the nation by building beautiful buildings, developing the arts of the artisans, and increasing commerce. Both had tried to find a short route to the Indies, and both had built up the navy as well as the army. As Alfred had founded Oxford, so Charles became a second founder in that he restored it when it was about to perish. Under both kings literature had been revived from a state of

IN LITERATURE 117

neglect. Indeed, according to Walker, Charles is a king equally celebrated and is the " true and natural heir " of the great Saxon ruler.

With the growth of Catholicism in England and the increasing dissatisfaction with the king, there arose a nostalgic yearning for the days of the Tudors. Andrew Marvell gave an early expression of this sentiment in his *An Historical Poem:*

> This Isle was well reform'd, and gain'd renown,
> Whilst the brave Tudors wore th'imperial crown:
> But since the royal race of Stuarts came,
> It has recoil'd to Popery and shame;
> Misguided monarchs, rarely wise or just,
> Tainted with pride, and with impetuous lust.

In *Britannia and Raleigh* he has Britannia relate how she called up " fam'd Spencer "

> In lofty notes Tudor's blest race to sing;
> How Spain's proud powers her virgin arms control'd,
> And gold'n days in peaceful order roul'd.

Accompanying this feeling there was a revival of interest in British story. Dryden in 1672 revived Carlell's *Arviragus and Philicia* and in his effort to support Charles, conceived the idea of using the Arthurian story to popularize the Stuart rule. The outcome of this attempt and the contradictory usage by Blackmore in defense of the Revolution will be discussed in the chapter devoted to Arthur as epic subject. The Honorable Edward Howard also wrote a British heroic poem entitled *The British Princes,* following his *Usurper,* a tragedy published in 1668. In 1678 there appeared anonymously an historical novel in two parts, *Tudor, a Prince of Wales,* and a few years later Chamberlayne's *Pharonnida* reappeared as a prose novel under the title of *Eromena or the Noble Stranger.* John Banks's *Destruction of Troy,* licensed January 29, 1679, relates in the prologue the story of the Trojan settlement of England after the fall of Troy and the building of Troy-novant. The spectators in the pit are even addressed as " London Trojans." It is in this association of the nation with the Trojans that the dramatist expects to find popularity for his account of the fall of Troy, the subject of the play itself.

The new interest in the British and especially the political employment of the Arthurian story necessitated a revival of the championship of the historicity of Arthur, particularly in the face of the open doubt expressed by such important figures as Milton and Stillingfleet. Crouch, always quick to sense the public demand, in 1687 wrote in avowed " vindication of our hero." He gave emphasis to his faith by placing his defense in a volume entitled the *History of the Nine Worthies,* in which Arthur is as authentic as the other unquestioned Worthies. He is named as the seventh Worthy and the first of the three Christian Worthies, Arthur, Charlemagne, and Godfrey. The account of Arthur covers some twenty pages and is prefaced by a conventional picture of the hero wearing his crown and bearing his sword in his hand. Under the picture is a

brief rhymed account of the accomplishments of Arthur.
There follows a prose defense of this Worthy against
those who " are of Opinion that there never was such
a Person " or who think " that all which hath been
written of his heroick Deeds, is meer Fiction and Invention." Crouch speaks out in no uncertain terms:

But as it is most execrable Infidelity to doubt that there was
a *Joshua,* wicked Atheism to question if there were a *David,*
and unreasonable to deny the being of *Judas Maccabeus*; as
it may be judged Folly to affirm there was never any *Alexander,*
Julius Caesar, Godfrey of *Boloigne* or *Charlemagne*; so we
may be thought guilty of Incredulity and Ingratitude, to
deny or doubt the honourable Acts of our victorious *Arthur.*

The account of Arthur's victories over the Saxons is
very concisely given. Some rather interesting additions
are made to the usual story: it is told how Occa, the
Saxon general, though desperately wounded, escaped
by ship to Germany; how the victorious Arthur offered
pardon to the Saxons if " they would turn Christians."
Such details as Arthur's single-handed destruction of
eight hundred Saxons in one battle, or the exact loca-
tion of each of the twelve set battles against the Saxons,
or the expedition to the continent, Crouch lists as
" questionable Matters." He includes, however, as
" more certain " a marvelous tale of Arthur's encounter
with the Scots and Picts in which Arthur lost his life
and Guinevere with many of her ladies was taken pris-
oner. This defeat was accompanied by many prodigies
of nature. The account closes with the story of the

finding of the bodies of Arthur and Guinevere buried at Glastonbury and Roscock's translation of Leland's epitaph for Arthur. The use of this epitaph points back definitely to a time when the story of Arthur was accepted and reports of such personal investigators as Leland were taken as unquestionable evidence. The popularity of this *History of the Nine Worthies* is attested by the fact that there were other editions in 1696, 1697, and 1700, respectively.

An earlier book by Crouch, *The Wonderful Curiosities, Rarities, and Wonders in England, Scotland, and Ireland* (1682), though in prose, is built upon a scheme much like Drayton's *Polyolbion* and contains a large amount of Arthurian legend. Crouch gives an account of the various sections of the country, incorporating the Arthurian associations with each place. When he tells of Hampshire, for instance, he includes the founding of the order of the Round Table, gives the names of some of the knights, and states that the Round Table preserved at Winchester could not be Arthur's. Under Cornwall he gives a sketch of Arthur's life and deeds, using without acknowledgment Fuller's account from the *Worthies,* with only a few minor changes in wording. Other editions of this work followed in 1685 and 1697.

The significance of Crouch's work becomes more apparent when we realize that he wrote against Popery; that in his *History of two late Kings James II and Charles II* his attitude is prejudiced; that at the time when the plot against William of Orange was brewing, he wrote a *History of Cromwell,* upholding the rights of revolution and a *History of the House of Orange,* showing William in a most favorable light. It has been said of Crouch that " his talent lies at collection "; we may add, I think, that his genius consisted in a feeling for the general interest of the public and an ability to satisfy this need in small, readable, and instructive volumes.

A play based upon British story, *Boadicea, Queen of Britain,* closed the century with a favorable portrayal of the British. Boadicea sets the tone of the play when she says, " No *Britain* born, can servilely obey." Pride of race and of country are shown throughout the play, and Cassibelan expresses the spirit of national independence characteristic of the British:

> Nature has made us for our selves alone.
> She fix'd our Isle, cast the wide Seas around,
> Made the strong Fence, and shall not hands be found
> In *Britain* to maintain the *British* bound?

One is hardly aware that in the end the Romans really overcome Cassibelan, for his spirit is unconquerable, and the British are portrayed as victorious until the fifth act. Local color is given by the worship of Boadicea and her two daughters at the temple, the songs of the Druids, and the use of auguries.

The study of the literature of the century substantiates the conclusion of the preceding chapter that British

material was superseded by Saxon during the Commonwealth, that it had a brief revival with the Restoration,
and that at the close of the century it was associated
with the Revolution and once more had considerable
popularity.

CHAPTER FOUR

ARTHUR AS EPIC SUBJECT

JONSON

In recounting Arthurian story in the *Polyolbion,*
Drayton had been impressed by its epic possibilities and
had suggested the theme as a fruitful one which would
do honor to the nation:

> For some abundant brain, oh, there had been a story,
> Beyond the blind man's might to have enhanced our glory.

It is of interest to note that the epic treatment of Arthurian story engaged the minds of all the great poets of
the seventeenth century except Donne. As widely diver-
gent types of genius as Jonson, Milton, and Dryden
felt the lure of the material. Each of these poets
planned its epic treatment, but not one of them carried
out his plan; and it was not until the end of the century
that Blackmore undertook with gigantic egotism to ful-
fill this ideal of the poets.

Whether Jonson got the idea of an Arthurian epic
from Drayton, whom he greatly admired, or from his
own investigation of the story for use in the entertainment for *Prince Henry's Barriers,* we know that he
was definitely considering the subject in 1619. In his
Conversations with Drummond he states that:

He had ane jntention to perfect ane Epick Poeme jntitled Heroölogia, of the Worthies of his Country rowsed by fame, and was to dedicate it to his Country.

We also know that he was more interested in Arthur than in any other hero whom he may have considered a Worthy of England and that he said, " for a Heroik poeme . . . there was no such ground as King Arthur's fiction." Two things are noticeable here in addition to the high regard in which he held Arthurian matter: one is that he acknowledged the story to be fiction; the other, that it is *King* Arthur, the defender of England, not *Prince* Arthur, the romantic hero portrayed by Spenser, in whom Jonson is interested. Indeed, it seems certain that none of the romances associated with Arthur and his knights would have had a place in Jonson's work. " Spenser's matter," he tersely said, " pleased him not." In *Prince Henry's Barriers* of 1609 he had stated that times were changed and that the old order of chivalry had passed. This attitude he reiterated in *Underwoods* LXII, *An Execration upon Vulcan,* when he consigned to the fire together with " Merlin's marvils "

> . . . the whole sum
> Of errant knighthood, with the dames and dwarfs;
> The charmed boats, and the enchanted wharfs,
> The Tristrams, Lancelots, Turpins, and the peers,
> All the mad Rolands and sweet Olivers.

In the *New Inn* Lovel praises Lord Beauford because

" he had no Arthurs " or other romances, but devoted
his time to the Greek and Roman epics. The romances
are disparagingly termed

> Abortives of the fabulous dark cloyster,
> Sent out to poison courts and infest manners.

He ridicules the long British pedigrees in *Staple of
News* and has Carlo Buffone in *Every Man Out of His
Humour* protest against " a tedious chapter of courtship,
after Sir Lancelot and queen Guenever," though he is
so well acquainted with Arthurian story that when Sog-
liardo and Shift enter in Act IV, scene 4, he dubs them
Sir Dagonet and his Squire. Jonson went so far as to
plan the verse form for his epic. He did not like Spenser's stanza; Drayton pleased him; he would write in
couplets, " for he detesteth all other Rimes." Why did
not Jonson, who was court poet for a monarch who
claimed double British ancestry, and who made other
use of Arthurian story, execute the work which he
appears seriously to have considered? Does not the
answer lie in the political situation following the year
in which Jonson had declared his intention of writing
an epic poem? It was in 1620, it will be remembered,
that matters reached a crisis between the king and
Parliament, and the interest of the learned circle in
which Jonson moved had turned Saxon. The time for
the popularity of an Arthurian epic had passed, and
Jonson was intimate enough with the situation to per-
ceive this fact.

MILTON

It has often been stated that Milton is the figure in whom the changing temper from Renaissance to seventeenth century is most clearly marked. This statement is especially true of Milton's attitude toward Arthurian story. In Milton we see exemplified that conflict between British and Saxon interest shown by the nation at large. In his young manhood Milton, unlike Jonson, had been fascinated by romance, as he tells us in the autobiographical passage in the *Apology,* and was strongly under the influence of Spenser, so that the romantic elements of Arthurian story had a very natural appeal. His change of feeling toward the subject and final abandonment of it, on the other hand, show him accepting the point of view of his own age. The history of this change makes an unusually interesting study.

By the time Milton was twenty, he showed in *A Vacation Exercise* that he was considering an epic subject " Of kings and queens and heroes old." From other early writings we learn the period in which he was interested and two of the subjects that he was seriously considering, the founding of the nation by Brute and the story of Arthur. The first is mentioned only once; the second is referred to several times and is sufficiently elaborated to show that he had in mind how the subject might be developed. In *To Manso* he expresses himself as longing for a patron like Manso should he ever write an English epic of " the kings of my native land, and Arthur, who carried war even into fairyland." He develops the idea yet further:

Or I shall tell of those great-hearted champions bound in the invisible society of the Round Table, and (O may the spirit be in me!) I shall break the Saxon phalanxes with British war.

In the *Epitaphium Damonis* he plans to begin his epic with the settlement of England by the Trojans, to tell of the colonization of Armorica and of the birth of Arthur, and finally, " to shrill forth the strains of my native land, and the cry of Britons in battle." Two years later when Milton is setting down a list of subjects from British history, the name of Arthur does not appear. About the same time, however, he states in *Of Reformation in England* that if he should choose the epic form for his great work, the subject should be taken from British history. Approximately a year later in *Reason of Church Government* he shows that he thinks of " our own ancient stories " as a fruitful field for epic subjects, and is considering " what king or knight before the conquest might be chosen in whom to lay the pattern of a Christian hero." Since Arthur was considered the third Christian Worthy and was British, since the other two Christian Worthies, Godfrey and Charlemagne, had already been used as epic subjects, and since Milton is under the influence of Spenser, it is natural to expect that he would eventually treat the Arthurian story. But when, after writing the divorce tracts, he could turn for a time from controversy, it was not in an epic but in the *History of Britain* that he became engaged. Here, as we shall see below, he presents very little concerning Arthur, and marks his treatment by out-spoken skepticism. When he finally writes the great epic of which he had dreamed so long, Arthur is not forgotten, but the references to him are used only to adorn this " graver subject " in the same manner as are the legends from the classics. There are two such passages in *Paradise Lost* and one in *Paradise Regained*, very lovely in themselves and rich in their connotation of the glamor of old romance. The first of these is in *Paradise Lost* in the passage where allusion to classical stories and romantic tales is made in the effort to give some idea of the number and power of Satàn's host:

> . . . and what resounds
> In fable or romance of Uther's son,
> Begirt with British and Armoric knights.

Here in brief compass is the Arthurian part of the epic outline suggested in the *Epitaphium*. Though Arthur is not definitely named in Milton's allusion to epic subjects in the autobiographical passage of Book IX, all the details which would have been necessary for the treatment of such a subject are repudiated: wars, " fabled knights in battles feigned," races, games, jousts, tournaments, feasts, the elaborate costumes and customs of chivalry. The last reference to Arthur is found in the second book of *Paradise Regained*, and is truly the stuff of poetry. The beauty of the maidens of Arthurian romance is used to bring out by comparison the greater loveliness of those classical attendant spirits for the banquet that Satan has prepared for Christ:

> . . . that seemed
> Fairer than feigned of old, or fabled since
> Of faery damsels met in forest wide
> By knights of Logres, or Lyones
> Lancelot, or Pelleas, or Pellenore.

Here we have recurrence to the theme sketched in *Mansus,* the stories of " those great-hearted champions bound in the invisible society of the Round Table "; but the sources are now Malory and Spenser, not British history. In these passages we see Milton illustrating the use to which poets could " by their art " put the fabulous and legendary material of their native land, the use that he suggested in his history; but a serious or extended treatment of Arthurian matter had become impossible to him.

In 1639 Milton clearly expressed his choice of an Arthurian subject; when he came to write his *History of Britain,* it is evident that his whole attitude toward both Arthur and the British had changed, and we never again hear of Arthur as an epic subject. Various explanations have been offered for this change. Each of these explanations is probably a part of the story; none of them seems sufficient to explain the fundamental alteration in opinion which the history reveals. MacCallum says, " First and chiefly, it may have been that in busying himself with the material, he did not find it sufficiently authenticated," and adds that Milton's " growing Puri-

tanism " led him to look " askance at fictions "; Verity
holds the same idea, feeling it to be impossible for
Milton to " build a long work on what he found to be
mainly fiction," but also suggests Milton's " increasing
Republicanism," which would have unfitted him for
writing about a great monarch; Hanford thinks that
" the historical material probably surprised him by its
richness, and it is not strange that we hear no more
of the Arthurian epic after the time when Milton had
become deeply interested in the non-legendary part of
English story "; Grierson also suggests that it is in part
the legendary quality of the story and in part Milton's
interest in his own great age rather than in the past
which account for his giving up the Arthurian epic, but
sees even more reason in his Puritan and anti-Catholic
ideas.

Certainly when Milton wrote his history he showed
a noticeably skeptical position toward Arthur. The
strange birth of the British national hero, his gigantic
prowess, the formation of the Round Table, the exploits
of the knights—legends suitable for elaboration in
romance—are not even mentioned. Wherever Arthur
is brought into the story, the sources for the material
are carefully cited, and facts are offered by Milton himself to cast doubt upon the narrative. In the first reference to Arthur he is mentioned as " Chief General for
the British Kings." The source given is Nennius, usually considered the most reliable of the early authorities,
but called by Milton " a very trivial writer." Milton

adds, however, concerning Arthur that he is "more renown'd in Songs and Romances, then in True stories," and cites proof from the invasions and victories of the Saxons at this time to show the impossibility of Arthur's attainments being such as he is credited with. In the next reference, a discussion of the Badon Hill victory, we find Milton expressing still greater skepticism and supporting this opinion with very convincing evidence. His statement could not be clearer:

But who *Arthur* was, and whether ever any such reign'd in *Britan*, hath bin doubted heertofore, and may again with good reason.

The attribution of the victory to Arthur is given on the authority of "such Authors as we have to follow." These are Nennius and Geoffrey, for whom, as we have seen, Milton shows very little regard. He points out that none of the writers nearest Arthur's time "whose credit hath sway'd most with the learneder sort" know anything of "this Arthur" beyond the account of Nennius, and shows how strange it is that Geoffrey's *Historia* should be the only book mentioning Arthur, "of whom . . . all other Histories were silent, both Forein and Domestic." The later writers are also neatly demolished; they "have sought to assert him by old Legends and Cathedral regests," but says Milton, "He who can accept of Legends for good story, may quickly swell a volume with trash, and had need be furnish'd with two only necessaries, leasure and beleif, whether it be the writer, or he that shall read." Arthur's parentage is next shown doubtful " since we read it not in certain story, that ever such person liv'd," the only authority being Geoffrey. His " puissance " is also shown to be questionable by such excellent evidence as the uncertainty of the Badon Hill victory, the story that Guinevere was kept a year by Melvas, whom Arthur could not conquer, by the fact that the Saxons " gained on him everywhere," and by the additional fact that the time sequence of the supposed events of Arthur's career is impossible. So, says Milton, "There will remain neither place nor circumstance in story, which may administer any liklihood of those great Acts that are ascribed to him." Milton dismisses the whole subject as too unimportant longer to interrupt the story and saying, " but not furder to contest about such uncertainties," he passes on to other matters.

Not only is Milton skeptical as to the historicity of Arthur, but he is also anti-British in his attitude. He even hurries over the story of the British, covering the period before the coming of the Romans in less than twenty-seven pages, and the entire period before the Saxon Heptarchy in less than half of the space devoted to the Saxons from then until their final overthrow. Everywhere the barbarity of the British is stressed. In the battle with the Romans under Suetonius they show themselves " right *Barbarians;* no rule, no foresight, no forecast, experience or estimation, either of themselves, or of thir Enemies; such confusion, such impotence, as seem'd likest not to a Warr, but to the wild hurrey of a

distracted Woeman, with as mad a Crew at her heels."
Their cruelty is emphasized as in the account of the
massacre of the Romans, where he states " no crueltie
that either outrage, or the insolence of success putt into
thir heads, was left unacted," and gives examples of
their barbaric practices and pagan reveling. The people
loved Vortigern, not for any virtues, but " because his
vices sorted so well with theirs," for he was " covetous,
lustful, luxurious, and prone to all vice." At the time
of Vortigern, Milton states on the authority of Gildas,
" few or none were likely to be other than lew'd and
wicked persons." Portraying kings that were incestuous
and people that were in a state of " general corruption "
in private and public life alike, Milton is giving not
only a realistic picture devoid of all the softening
touches of romance, but is also revealing a definite prej-
udice against the British. These, he says, are " Progeni-
tors not to be glori'd in."

Milton's attitude toward the Saxons, on the other
hand, is far different. In the first place, he regards the
material as sufficiently important for it to be worth
while for him to sift evidence, to reconcile the various
accounts, and to weigh authorities—a task he scorned in
the British period as useless since little of the whole
story was true—in order that he may reach a logical and
continuous history of events. He is willing to undergo
this, though " what labour is to be endur'd . . . is a
penance to think." The development of learning in this
period and the growth of civilization present a strong

contrast to the barbarity of the British, and form, no doubt, one of the grounds of Milton's interest in the Saxons. The good qualities of the Saxon rulers are stressed whenever possible: Ethelbert is praised as a " favorer of all civility" and the " giver of laws"; Edwin makes the nation safe, and " to his Faith adding Vertue, by the due administration of Justice wrought such peace over all his Territories, that from Sea to Sea, Man or Woman might have travail'd in safety." His praise of Alfred is naturally high, for Milton admires him for his system of laws, his thirst after knowledge, his efforts in behalf of learning, and his " exact Justice." Alfred, in contrast with Vortigern, spends his time " not idely or voluptuously, but in all vertuous imploy-ments both of mind and body." He is called the " Mirror of Princes," and his work is termed "those many glorious labours of his Life both in Peace and War." When it becomes necessary to recount the decline of the Saxons, he makes excuse for the relation, saying that it is " not to blur or taint the praises of thir former Actions and Liberty well defended."

It is evident, then, from an examination of Milton's history that Milton is aggressively skeptical about Arthur, that he is anti-British in sympathy, and that he presents the most favorable portrayal of the Saxons that his material will allow. How are we to account for this new position?

Milton's skepticism is undoubtedly in part attribut-able to the growing skepticism of the seventeenth cen-

tury. It is far more significant, however, to note that by
the time Milton undertook his history he had taken his
stand with Parliament and its ancient Saxon rights and
against the tyranny of Charles I, with whom was still
associated the British legend in spite of Powell's attempt
to draw a parallel between Charles and Alfred. The
legend which had supported Tudor absolutism could not
now be used by Milton. It is noteworthy that this is the
only fable which Milton takes pains to refute, for he
recognizes that all early history is " obscur'd and blem-
isht with Fables," and that there are several reasons for
not discarding all fabulous stories: some authors of
judgment and learning accept as fact that which others
hold to be fabulous; things held to be fabulous are
sometimes found " to contain in them many footsteps
of something true "; and finally, these stories are of
value for the poets. He does not, therefore, wholly
reject the legend of Brutus, and his history is a rich
storehouse of fable.

We have already seen in Chapter Two that Milton's
interest in Saxon ideas and his use of Saxon law in support of the Commonwealth naturally led to his stand
against the British. These, however, do not complete
the explanation of Milton's repudiation of the British.
In the parallel drawn at the beginning of Book III
between the failure of the Commonwealth and the defi-
ciency of the British in using their liberty after the
departure of the Romans, we find another striking clue
to Milton's rejection of the British story. " The late

Civil Broils," he says, " had cast us into a condition not much unlike to what the *Britans* then were in." In both periods " glorious liberty " had been put into the hands of the people, and in both the great struggle for freedom had been brought to " ridiculous frustration." In his own time " the like defects, the like miscarriages notoriously appear'd, with vices not less hateful or inexcusable." The English like the British before them had shown themselves " valiant indeed, and prosperous to win a field; but to know the end and reason of winning, injudicious and unwise; in good and bad success alike unteachable." Milton had given up for an indefinite period the life work for which he had been unremittedly preparing, in order to fight for liberty—to him a sacred cause—and now sees that the whole struggle with its " many labours, much bloodshed, and vast expense " had been in vain. The monarchy had been overthrown, but " the heroick Wisdom which is required " rightly to use liberty was far above the grasp of these " narrow Polliticians." Like the early Britans they found themselves enmeshed in things " too hard and generous above thir straine and temper," and found their liberty a burden too oppressive for them. Milton is looking at his own age with disillusioned eyes. He gives a bitter picture of the times following the success of the civil war:

But when once the superficiall zeal and popular fumes that acted thir New Magistracy were cool'd, and spent in them, strait every one betook himself (setting the Commonwealth behind, his private ends before) to doe as his own profit or ambition ledd him.   Then was justice delay'd, and soon after deni'd: spight and favour determin'd all: hence faction, thence treachery, both at home and in the field: ev'rywhere wrong, and oppression: foull and horrid deeds committed daily, or maintain'd in secret or in open.

A new sort of oppression is set up, and men " huckster the Commonwealth " for their own good, even if it necessitates playing into the hands of the enemy. Those in political life are hypocritical, scorning no means for personal safety or for gain; those in the church are no better, for the " Reformation " has served only to enable the reformers to indulge in the same sins as those from which they pretended to have reformed the church: lack of learning and indifference to truth, avarice, covetous-ness, time-serving, holding of pluralities, and spiritual tyranny. The disciples of the churchmen act both blindly and stupidly and are like " Children of the Devil." Between the Church and the laity " there hath not been a more ignominious and mortell wound to Faith, to Piety, to the work of the Reformation." History had repeated itself and the same faults of which the British had been guilty recurred in both Church and State.

It is the study of the successive periods of history which leads a nation to an understanding of herself, and self-knowledge Milton considers even more impor-tant for a nation than for a private man. The reason for the parallel between the British period and his own age is that " we may be able from two such remarkable turns of state, producing like events among us, to raise a knowledge of ourselves both great and weighty." Like Bolton, Milton would block out his history into epochs, and like Selden he would study the past for the light that it throws upon the present. This is what he means by saying that his purpose in writing history is " to instruct and benefit them that read," and that his task is a serious one, necessitating a prayer for " divine assistance, that it may redound to his glory and the good of the British nation." Milton sees more in a survey of history than the Calvinistic conception of the hand of God rewarding the good and punishing the evil. The responsibility for the changing fortunes of the nation lies in the nature of the English people, who do not know how to use liberty. Given liberty, they quickly turn it into license and bring about a renewal of subjection. There is an inseparable bond between virtue and liberty, but " civility, prudence, love of the Publick good, more then of money or vaine honour, are to this soile in a manner outlandish." This is a teaching which leads toward *Paradise Lost* and not toward an Arthurian epic.

With the new science, furthermore, had come an upheaval in thought of which we today can scarcely conceive. Spenser and Donne expressed the resulting disharmony and doubt. Unable to find a system of cosmic order, Spenser set forth his doubts and questionings in a theory of mutability. Donne could not reconcile his faith in God with the new science and attempted to escape the conflict in his mind by doubting nature rather

than God. Milton was not satisfied to leave matters
unsolved. He attempted to reconcile these doubts and
questionings and find an ordered universe through the
conception that all is a part of the great plan of God.
Such a philosophy could not, of course, be applied to
the Arthurian legend, though it could well be embodied
in the story of the fall of man.

In writing on the subject of *Paradise Lost,* Milton
gave the most complete expression of his own age which
his genius could devise. In such an attempt he was
following the example of the other great epic writers:
Virgil incorporated in a narrative of the fall of Troy
the life of his own times; Tasso gave to the account of
Godfrey those chivalric ideas which had developed
through the succeeding centuries and blossomed in contemporary life; Spenser used the legend of Arthur to
picture life in the Renaissance. Bacon strikes to the core
of this poetic ideal when he says that, " Poetry is the
accommodation of the shows of things to the desires of
the mind." To Spenser as the poet of Elizabeth's reign
the Golden Age was the Arthurian period; to Milton
as the poet of the Commonwealth the Golden Age was
a renewed Paradise. About the time that he was making the four drafts for the dramatic treatment of the
Paradise Lost theme, he wrote of his own time that it is
" the age of ages " with God standing at the door. He
believes that a Golden Age in both religion and government is at hand: he is sure that God will perfect the
work of the Reformation and bring " settled peace in

the Church and righteous Judgment in the Kingdom ";
he feels that England is a chosen nation and dreams of
a Commonwealth in which there will be complete liberty
of the individual—a new age of freedom, justice, and
peace. For these blessings " every true protested Brittain " is called upon in the *Animadversions* to " render
thanks to God the Father of Light, and fountain of
heavenly Grace, and to his Son Christ our Lord." In
the wonderful prayer which closes *Of Reformation in
England* he had already suggested that when that age
arrives, " some one may perhaps be heard offering at
high strains in new and lofty measure to sing and celebrate thy divine mercies and marvellous judgments in
this land throughout all ages." It is this spirit of
expectant joy and thanksgiving that Milton composes
his hymn to light (if we accept the testimony of Philips
for the date of these lines), which is later incorporated
in his story of the Garden of Eden. For the restoration
of such a Golden Age Milton is willing to make any
sacrifice, whether it be to speak in " plain ungarnish't
prose," or to give up his sight. With the failure of the
Commonwealth the likeness of his own age to the biblical story which he had studied for its dramatic qualities
became so striking that it seemed as though the account
of the fall of man embodied the joy, the despair, and
the consoling hope of contemporary times. The Golden
Age of liberty had been once more in the hands of
man; once more man showed that he did not know how
" rightly to use liberty," but let his reason sink sub-

servient to his human passions; immediately there sprang up a train of " inordinate desires " such as followed the fall of man, and the precious gift of liberty was lost. When finally Milton turned to his ideal work, it was with the realization that *Paradise Lost,* not the legend of Arthur, was the true expression of his age and that it revealed the justification of " the ways of God to man " in the course of history as well as in the life of the individual.

Milton's rejection of the Arthurian legend is, therefore, seen to be a far more complex matter than merely a distaste for fiction. His knowledge of the barbarity of the British, his recognition that any complete poetic expression of contemporary times would necessarily cover not only the glory of the Britons but also their degradation and would leave him without a triumphant hero, his interest in the greater civilization of the Saxons and especially in the laws which had figured so largely in recent history, his repudiation of the absolutism of the Tudors and Stuarts, who had used the Arthurian legend to strengthen their rights, and his attempt to show order in the universe and a divine plan which would explain the seeming mutability in its affairs—all these combine to lead Milton away from the story of Arthur and to center his choice upon the theme of *Paradise Lost.*

DRYDEN

Once again the Arthurian subject was to come under consideration for epic treatment by a great poet. In his preface to the translation of Juvenal, Dryden states that it had been his intention to discontinue writing plays and to undertake a work for the honor of his country which would engage him the remainder of his life. This was to be an epic of " king Arthur, conquering the Saxons " or of the Black Prince. The subject of King Arthur appealed to him because " being farther distant in Time " it " gives the greater scope to my Invention." Whichever subject he chose, however, he intended to imitate Virgil and Spenser in representing " living Friends and Patrons of the noblest Families " and in shadowing " the Events of future Ages in the Succession of our Imperial Line." In working out his plan for this epic, Dryden had devised a means for elevating the modern epic to the height of the ancient by the use of the " Guardian Angels of the Kingdoms " for supernatural machinery. In a letter to Dennis he calls this device a " better Hint for new Machines " than the Christian epic afforded in the use of God and the devil. The " Guardian Angels of the Kingdoms," however, " are not to be touch'd by every Hand," for they demand a knowledge of " Platonick Philosophy."

Unlike Milton, Dryden gave up his Arthurian epic from no sense of conviction but purely because of financial inability to devote the time to it. It was necessary for him to continue the more profitable occupation of writing plays. The subject retained its interest for him, however, and we find him adapting it to dramatic opera, patterned after *The Tempest,* which Dryden terms

" tragedy mixed with opera." Dryden's *King Arthur*
was written with a definite political purpose and was to
be produced to strengthen the power of Charles II; but
it was so delayed in production that it did not appear
until after William and Mary came to the throne, and,
therefore, had to be revised until it was unrecognizable.
In the dedication to the Marquis of Halifax, Dryden
himself says in regard to the changes:

But, not to offend the present times, nor a government which
has hitherto protected me, I have been obliged so much to
alter the first design, and take away so many beauties from
the writing, that it is now no more what is was formerly,
than the present ship of the Royal Sovereign, after so often
taking down and altering, is the vessel it was at the first
building.

These were ticklish times, and Dryden's work was
closely scrutinized because, as Scott points out in his
remarks concerning *Cleomenes,* Dryden's " well-known
skill at adapting an ancient story to a modern moral had
so often been exercised in the cause of the House of
Stuart." *Cleomenes,* in fact, was censored by Queen
Mary for its reference to an exiled monarch who sought
aid on the continent and for other details which were
considered to represent the affairs of the Stuarts. *The
Prophetess* with its references to the " Irish war, female
regency, and Revolution " was also suppressed. Since
the *Duke of Guise,* which immediately preceded *King
Arthur,* was a political play representing the Duke of

Monmouth by Guise, it was also forbidden. The original political nature of *King Arthur* may be judged by *Albion and Albanius,* of which the first act was written as a prologue to *King Arthur* and often practiced "before the king at Whitehall." When the performance of the main design was deferred by "some intervening accidents," Dryden states that he wrote two more acts to the prologue and made it a complete entertainment in itself. *Albion and Albanius* in its three-act form was performed on June 3, 1685. As in the *Duke of Guise* the allegory is unmistakable. Charles is Albion; the Duke of York, Albanius; the purpose of the play is to show the victory of the crown. The events following the Restoration, the death of Charles, and the accession of James are all plainly represented. It is this kind of treatment which Dryden used in the first writing of the Arthurian story. When *King Arthur* finally appeared in 1691, all the real substance of the story had been removed, and what remained was only a fantastic account of Arthur's battle with the Saxons.

When the opera opens, Arthur has been victorious in ten of his great battles with the Saxons and is facing another struggle on St. George's day. Both Oswald, the Saxon leader, and Arthur are in love with the blind daughter of the Duke of Cornwall, but she has been promised to Arthur. Oswald, however, captures Emmeline, and Arthur challenges Oswald to single combat. Arthur disarms Oswald and wins Emmeline, who has her sight restored by some of Merlin's magic drops. The supernatural machinery is provided by magicians. Merlin, throughout the conflict with the Saxons, intervenes in Arthur's behalf; Osmond, a Saxon magician, and Grimbald, " a fierce earthy spirit," aid the Saxons. Philidel, a dainty Ariel-like being not yet fully tarnished by his stay in hell, connects the two supernatural groups and is the finest creation in the opera. Escaping from Grimbald, he is taken into the service of Merlin and keeps the British army from being led astray into bogs by the deception of Grimbald. Later, also, he defeats the magic of Osmond. By Osmond's power the forest through which Arthur must approach the Saxon fort is enchanted, after the pattern set by Tasso, with an evil spirit under every leaf. The terror of this living wood inhabited by many fearful animals and full of dire noises, drives back Arthur's forces. Merlin, however, finds a way to counter Osmond's enchantment sufficiently for Arthur to reach Emmeline, who is imprisoned in the wood. There ensues a charming scene in which Emmeline with sight restored sees Arthur for the first time. Emmeline is held by charms too strong even for Merlin's art, and Arthur and Merlin have to flee the approaching Osmond, leaving Emmeline behind. Osmond, infuriated to find that Arthur and Merlin have penetrated the forest, sets still more impregnable spells and subjects Arthur to the temptations of the flesh. Entertained by soft music, lovely sirens, dancers, and singers, his senses respond. Finally, Grimbald, disguised as Emmeline, appeals to his passion. Fully aware that it will be in violation of the control of reason to be "fondly overcome by female charm" as was Milton's Adam, Arthur choses to dispense with rational control:

> By thy leave, reason, here I throw thee off,
> Thou load of life.

Arthur is saved, however, by Philidel, who reveals to Arthur that it is Grimbald whom he is about to embrace. He then binds Grimbald and enables Arthur to complete the disenchantment of the grove. Nothing here suggests Geoffrey, old Arthurian legend, or contemporary political allegory; only a fairy story remains.

In noting the loss to literature occasioned by the fact that neither Milton nor Dryden carried out his original plan to write an Arthurian epic, Scott keenly remarks:

But Arthur, as a sort of counterpoise to his extravagant reputation during the middle ages, was doomed, in the seventeenth century, to be reluctantly abandoned by Milton and Dryden, and to be celebrated by the pen of Blackmore.

SIR RICHARD BLACKMORE

When the giants of the century abandoned the Arthurian subject, Sir Richard Blackmore, Physician in Ordinary to King William III, took it up. Even though Blackmore claimed that "the Business of my Profession . . . was then greater then at any time before," he found the writing of epics in twelve books each "an Innocent Amusement to entertain me in such leisure hours which were usually past away before in Conversation and unprofitable hearing and telling of News." Judicious friends tried to persuade him to write on " some useful Subject " in the field of medicine or philosophy, but thoughts of the necessary research irked him; epics could be composed without books around him, " in Coffee-houses, and in passing up and down the Streets." Sir Richard looked over the list of the great epic writers, decided that only Homer and Virgil had been successful in the field, and being convinced that " to write an Epick Poem is a work of that Difficulty, that no one for near seventeen hundred years past has succeeded in it," assumed his ability to rival Homer and Virgil by writing epics for " the Entertainment of my idle hours." Ariosto, Tasso, Spenser—these had not followed the rules: he would carefully observe the laws set forth by Aristotle and Horace, Rapin, Dacier, and Bossu—even Mr. Rymer—and become a seventeenth century Virgil. And so an Arthurian epic, which had seemed to Dryden the work of a lifetime and had been Milton's dream through years of preparation, was given to the world far out of its due season by a doctor of medicine! Blackmore's *Prince Arthur* of 1695, followed by *King Arthur* in 1700, brought to the physician a widespread fame, which, contrary to the opinion of his friends, his medical tracts such as his " Three discourses on the nature and cure of the cholick, melancholy, and palsies " would never have afforded.

SOURCES

GEOFFREY OF MONMOUTH

Blackmore found the basis for both his epics in the historical material offered by Geoffrey of Monmouth. As we have seen, this source had been largely discredited during the century, but with the Revolution the British story had once more found a place of importance in the consciousness of the nation, and Geoffrey was not without his strong defenders. Furthermore, Blackmore's purpose of depicting Arthur as both prince and king had its place in sending Blackmore to this source. Geoffrey contained some account of Arthur before he was crowned as well as the record of his great deeds after he became king, and that was the type of material which Blackmore needed for his portrayal of William of Orange as Arthur. Though Blackmore does not try to defend the historical accuracy of Geoffrey or the existence of Arthur, he states that he considers the *Historia* " sufficient Foundation for an Epick Poem." The *Prince Arthur* is not definitely referred to Geoffrey, but in various details and in the general account of Arthur's winning England from the Saxons it shows clearly enough upon what source Blackmore founded his epic. In the Preface to *King Arthur* Blackmore does attribute his material to Geoffrey and even recounts the main outlines of the story of Arthur's continental conquests as told by Geoffrey to show his authority for the incidents narrated.

A brief synopsis of the story of *Prince Arthur* seems necessary not only to show Blackmore's use of Geoffrey but also to reveal other indebtedness which will be discussed later. Though the opening of the story differs from Geoffrey, Arthur's battles with the Saxons, his march to London, and his victory over Ireland and Scotland are all based upon the account in the *Historia.* Arthur, who has taken refuge on the continent after the Saxons overcame Uther, is shown first on his way back to England with a large force to recover his crown. He is shipwrecked by a violent storm which has been raised by Satan with the aid of Thor, for Satan assists the Saxons, and is cast upon the Armorican shore. Encouraged by Raphael (for the heavenly forces are on Arthur's side) and assisted by Hoel's generous aid, Arthur repairs his ships and continues to England, where he is acclaimed with joy. The final six books are taken up with Arthur's conquest of the kingdom, including Ireland and Scotland, in spite of Satan's efforts to destroy the British army by the power of Asmodai and the Saxon treachery in violating the treaty which promised to Arthur the Saxon Princess Ethelina. After causing the Saxon army to fall like autumn leaves upon the field, Arthur engages the Saxon Tollo in single combat and wins both the Saxon Princess and the kingdom.

Virgil

From this brief summary it is evident that Blackmore in shaping his material by the Virgilian pattern, which, he says, " I look on as the most just and perfect, and which is most easily accommodated to the present Age, supposing the Christian Religion in the place of the Pagan." He makes no apology for his imitation of Virgil " in so many places of this Poem," holding that in doing so, he is following Virgil's example in imitating Homer. The statement of the theme is given in true Virgilian manner: " I sing the *Briton* and his righteous arms." The account of the cause of Juno's hate is paralleled by an analysis of Satan's hate for Arthur. Just as Juno seeks the region of storms and sues Aeolus for a fearful storm, so does Satan fly to Thor, the keeper of storms, for aid. Blackmore always thinks that he can improve upon what he imitates, and so depicts a storm that would doubtless have surprised Aeolus; the very poles are blown awry, and the earth is wrested " from its place." In Blackmore, Uriel takes Neptune's place as the one to calm the waves. In both stories the shipwrecked ones prepare an elaborate feast as soon as they reach land, and in both a messenger is sent to secure the protection of that part of the company that has become separated in the storm. As Venus appears to comfort Aeneas, so Raphael comes to encourage Arthur. Hoel is as favorably impressed with Arthur as Dido is with Aeneas and serves a feast at his court just as does Dido. At each feast the minstrel sings of creation. At Dido's request Aeneas relates the story of his past history; Lucius, a friend of Arthur, performs this function in Blackmore, for Arthur, having narrated the complete story of the Bible for two days on the way to Hoel's palace, is so tired that he excuses himself and goes to bed immediately after supper. The funeral games and the prizes form a model for the races in Blackmore, especially in that Blackmore follows Virgil very closely in giving the incident of the one who fails on account of an accident as a claimant for the prize. Hoel's sending a chariot to Arthur is undoubtedly modeled upon the gift of a chariot to Aeneas by King Latinus. Blackmore slavishly follows Virgil's account of Lavinia's being promised to Aeneas, in the betrothal of Ethelina to Arthur; of Turnus's breaking the treaty; and of the account of the princes who supported him. The ceremony with which the body of Pallas, covered with a rich and prized garment, the gift of Aeneas, is sent home is reproduced in the funeral of Macor. Blackmore also uses the detailed description of the shield (which might, of course, be from Homer), the councils of both gods and mortals, and the single combat in which victory is won. Whatever we may feel about the value of Blackmore's effort, we have to admit that he has made a very successful imitation.

SPENSER

The very titles of the two epics, *Prince Arthur* and *King Arthur,* send us straight to Spenser. In his letter to Raleigh, it will be remembered, Spenser pointed out Homer's use of separate books for the story of Ulysses (the virtuous man) and Agamemnon (the good governor), Virgil's combination of the two characters in

Aeneas, Ariosto's picture of both in Orlando, and Tasso's separate portrayal of them in two characters, Rinaldo and Godfrey, in one book. In this letter, also, Spenser stated his plan to

pourtraict in Arthure, before he was king, the image of a brave knight, perfected in the twelve private morall vertues, as Aristotle hath devised, which is the purpose of these first twelve bookes: which if I finde to be well accepted, I may be perhaps encoraged to frame the other part of polliticke vertues in his person, after hee came to be a king.

What Spenser had left incomplete was fertile field for the productive Blackmore, who not only felt competent to attempt the theme but also anticipated surpassing Spenser's method, for

Ariosto and Spenser . . . not observing this judicious Conduct of Virgil, nor attending to any sober Rules, are hurried on with boundless, impetuous Fancy over Hill and Dale, till they are both lost in a Wood of Allegories.

In his definition of the epic as given in the Preface to *Prince Arthur* he shows that he has the division of private and political virtues in mind: the hero is " some Valiant, or Wise, or Pious Prince, or great Commander."

Though he adopted Spenser's general scheme, Blackmore did not follow Spenser in embodying in a separate individual each of the private moral virtues. The starting point with Blackmore was a given action and a real character, whereas with Spenser both the character and the action had to be invented. The nature of Blackmore's historical material demanded that Arthur be the dominating character throughout the epic, showing in himself the embodiment of each princely virtue. Piety is given as his outstanding virtue. It is manifested not only by the fact that he is under heaven's especial care, but also by the application of the term *pious* some twenty odd times. One recalls, of course, pious Aeneas; it is more significant, however, that, as in Spenser, holiness is the first virtue portrayed and that Prince Arthur defeats the heathen Saxons, identified with the Catholics, a victory comparable to that of the Red Cross Knight over Error. Indeed, Arthur comes to restore " religion," by which is meant Protestantism, and is literally the Defender of the Faith. The crown is promised for the defense of the faith and as a symbol of his favor in the sight of heaven. Arthur has, therefore, the same general purpose as the Red Cross knight. Arthur's *courage* is second in prominence only to his piety, and he is called courageous, brave, valiant, almost as frequently as he is termed pious. In battle he is to be found in the places of greatest danger, and his resistless onslaught is repeatedly compared to that of the flood, or of fire in a parched forest, or of the raging tempest. Stirred by righteous indignation against the foe, he wields his mighty sword with such destructive force that " like grass mown down the slaughtered Saxons lay." In spite of his martial rage Arthur is always *magnanimous* when his foe speaks fairly, proposes terms, or makes a request. He is ever ready to listen and with great-souled generosity to make concessions that would tax the character of any ordinary man. He possesses qualities which win and hold *friendship;* he is perfectly just both to followers and foes, and can be counted upon to meet any situation with an open mind and to decide the issues with fairness; he never shirks responsibility, but always leads his men. He also gives to his followers a devotion as sincere as that which is bestowed upon him. Like Hrothgar of old Arthur *rewards* his companions in battle:

> Dispensing great Rewards thro' all the Host
> To those whose Courage was distinguish'd most.

It is he, too, who not only awards the prizes for the races with which his hosts amuse themselves in true English fashion in the monotony of a lull in battle, but also bestows rich gifts upon the losers. When Macor, his friend, lies dead, it is Arthur who throws over the bier a robe " Pond'rous with Orient Pearl, and stiff with Gold," his own gift from King Odar. Prince Arthur likewise has the virtue of *temperance.* When Asmodai, accompanied by Riot, Luxury, and Wine, invades Arthur's camp, Arthur alone remains untouched.

With this rich endowment of virtues attributed to Prince Arthur, what is there yet to add to distinguish the king from the prince? Blackmore might well have said, " One thing thou lackest." Upon the virtues of the private man he superimposes the supremacy of reason. This rule of reason is the characteristic which Aristotle points out as marking the ruler from others.

In order to demonstrate the qualities of the ruler, Aristotle makes an analogy between the rule of the soul over the body and the authority of the ruler over his subjects: " the virtue of the ruler we maintain to be different from that of the subject; the one being the virtue of the rational, and the other of the irrational part." Just what he means by the virtue of the rational is definitely stated in another passage: " And it is clear that the rule of the soul over the body, and the mind and the rational element over the passionate is natural and expedient; whereas the equality of the two or the rule of the inferior is always hurtful." Again he says: " If the ruler is intemperate and unjust, how can he rule well? . . . If he be licentious and cowardly, he will certainly not do his duty . . . Hence the ruler ought to have moral virtue in perfection, for his duty is entirely that of a master artificer, and the master artificer is reason."

If Blackmore is completing Spenser's plan for the treatment of Arthurian matter by portraying the political virtues in King Arthur, it is natural to suppose that he would go to Aristotle to find the distinguishing virtues of the ruler. Spenser's remark would suggest this source. Furthermore, the supremacy of reason, an idea stressed by the Stoics and especially emphasized by the neo-Stoics, was an idea which had pervaded the thought of the Renaissance and molded the heroes of those allegorical works which most influenced Blackmore. Tasso had made Understanding or Reason the supreme vir-

tue of Godfrey, the ruler, and had depicted this virtue
as an active force, meeting and overcoming trials of its
strength. Particularly had he set forth the temptation
of the senses through the power of Armida. Sidney,
too, in the *Arcadia* had drawn the private man and the
ruler. In the story of Pyrocles and Musidorus he sets
forth the " vertues of a private man "; in Evarchus he
especially illustrates the character of a wise ruler. By
both the negative evidence of what a ruler should not be
and the positive picture of what he should be, Sidney
makes clear that the ruler is a man whose actions are
dominated by reason. That Sidney accepts the idea that
reason should rule over the other faculties is revealed in
a number of passages. Musidorus states the principle
with great exactness:

Remember (for I know you know it) that if we will be men,
the reasonable parte of our soul, is to have absolute com-
maundement; against which if sensual weaknes arise, we are
to yeelde all our sounde forces to the overthrowing of so
unnaturall a rebellion.

This virtue, furthermore, is not to be " unbreathed,"
for Pyrocles and Musidorus set out with the definite
intention to exercise their virtues. If then, temperance in
the Platonic sense of the rational principle, is the highest quality of the private individual, how much more
necessary it is that the ruler shall be governed by this
principle. It is interesting to speculate what Sidney
would have done with the Arthurian material had he
followed out the intention which Jonson attributes to

him " to have transform'd all his Arcadia to the stories
of King Arthur." The Pyrocles-Musidorus material and
the treatment of Evarchus indicate that he would also
have used Prince Arthur to illustrate the private moral
virtues and have followed up this portrayal with that
of the king to depict the politic virtue. Spenser in Book
II of the *Faerie Queene* showed in Guyon that he
thought of Temperance as a positive force in man, a
force that could meet and overcome the temptations of
sense. It is not merely an " absence of excess, a golden
mean, but it is the control of all powers, mental desires
as well as physical desires, by the rational element in
the soul." Furthermore, Spenser shows not only temperance but all virtue in the process of developing
toward perfection. This development is brought about
by the active resistance of temptation and is a militant
conception. Such a philosophy strongly indicates that
Spenser's idea of a ruler would also have been that of
a person who above all others illustrates the control of
the rational over the irrational. Milton under Spenser's
influence makes the trial of reason the significant fact
in both the fall of man and the temptation of Christ.
Adam falls when sensual appetite overcomes the
rational principle:

> For Understanding ruled not, and the Will
> Heard not her lore, both in subjection now
> To sensual Appetite, who, from beneath
> Usurping over sovran Reason, claimed
> Superior sway.

Free to choose good or evil, warned by Raphael that Reason should be in control, Adam is unable to meet the active struggle between the rational and the irrational principles within him. In the three-fold temptation of Christ by Satan in *Paradise Regained* it is again the rational principle which is assailed, but Christ, being that very Son of God, is able to retain that perfect harmony of His powers which is possible only when Reason is in control.

Following this great tradition, what tests does Blackmore devise to establish the control of reason in King Arthur? By divine permission, as in the case of Job, Satan subjects Arthur for a period of fourteen days first, to all the horrors that hell can devise and second, to the enticements of the senses. These tests are set apart in a book which Blackmore marks out for especial notice by stating in the Preface: " I have in the Sixth Book adventur'd on an Allegory, finding Homer has done the like in his Story of Circe." Blackmore uses *allegory* in a similar sense when he says in his comment upon *Job* as an epic that Satan's appearance before God is allowed by the critics as allegory, and again in the Preface to *Prince Arthur* when he discusses the nature of epic poetry and speaks of the literal sense and the " Mystical or Typical Sense." Here he is following Harington, who in the preceding century had pointed out that there was in allegory a literal sense or story within which there was a moral sense " profitable for the active life of man, approving vertuous actions, and condemning the contrarie." The term allegory as applied to the Sixth Book of *King Arthur* is further explained in Blackmore's *Essay upon Epick Poetry:*

Vertues and Vices are represented as Persons either Humane or Divine, and proper Passions and Manners are ascrib'd to their respective characters.

Even " various Qualities of the Mind " may be thus represented. Such allegory elevates the poem, but he suggests that it must not be used too freely as in Ariosto and Spenser. Rather it is to be employed with " Temperance and Judgment." In restricting allegory to the above definition in this part of his epic, Blackmore is consciously relieving the mind from carrying the legend by which contemporary history is represented, so that the full significance of this central book of the epic may be more easily perceived. This is the story of Book VI. Satan, in desperation because of his fear of having to surrender Lutetia, dares to take his " faded Splendor " before the throne of God. He finds God holding audience with the Guardian Angels of the Kingdoms (Blackmore's only effort to incorporate Dryden's idea), who are reporting on terrestrial affairs. Satan is granted permission to test the " constancy " of Arthur, the only restriction being that he is not to touch Arthur's life, a restriction again reminiscent of Job. This permission granted, Satan, after his usual manner, raises a storm, shipwrecks Arthur on the Orkneys, and then when Arthur has gone apart on a mountain to pray, seizes upon him and bears him aloft in the air to a

waste place at the foot of a mountain. Here Arthur
fights with a very fearful dragon. Somewhat disgrun-
tled that Arthur meets the first test so well, Satan next
bears Arthur to an enchanted wood, like that portrayed
by Tasso or Dryden in his *King Arthur*. Horror is
heaped upon horror. Here the gloomy trees of pine,
cypress, yew, admit no light. All kinds of birds of ill
omen inhabit these trees, and poisonous plants grow
beneath them. Out of the darkness proceed horrible
mysterious sounds. He is confronted by " murd'ring
Ruffians," by Hell-hounds which " ran roaring on him
with their open Jaws," and by ghosts. Arthur
" unmov'd and ignorant of Fear " then comes to a castle in the midst of the wood. It is surrounded by a moat
of blood and is inhabited by a horrible monster with
vipers around her temples:

> Her shapeless Form no Words have force to tell,
> Black as the Night, and Horrible as Hell.

When Arthur approaches the castle, a drawbridge is let
down, and the monster appears, accompanied by a " hid-
eous Rout," whose distracted faces revealed " Consum-
mate Horror." Unable to daunt Arthur she flees back
into the castle:

> For she the timorous only can devour
> But flys the brave who dare resist her power.
>
> .   .   .   .
>
> None but the Brave conscious of Vertuous Deeds,
> Whose Courage from their Innocence proceeds,
> Are able to withstand her dreadful Power.

Angry at his continued defeat, Satan decides to change
his tactics to " a more fatal kind " and " Conquer by
Wiles whom Danger cannot shake." Accordingly, he
takes Arthur to a " flowry vale," in the midst of which
is a castle with its surrounding gardens, a place comparable to the Garden of Armida in Tasso or the Bower of
Bliss in Spenser. Among the fragrant flowers and herbs
of the garden appear ivory tables loaded with an entic-
ing banquet. Further to appeal to his senses is music
" exceeding that of the tuneful Sphears." A beautiful
blond, Fascinia, and her " wanton train " come forth
from the palace and urge Arthur to enjoy the feast,
diverting himself " with Pleasure's charming Voice "
after the dangers that he has undergone. The alluring
Fascinia, who offers the services of her nymphs and the
subjection of herself, has vanquished many "great
heroes " by " her gentle charms." When she speaks
with Arthur

> A thousand Graces, and a thousand Joys
> Smil'd in her Cheeks and danc'd within her Eyes.

Arthur responds to her sensual charms; his heart quick-
ens its beat, his blood flames, he is fired with love—
and he enjoys the sensation! But Fascinia, like Circe,
has the power to transform men into beasts, or women!
Arthur, who has been warned by an angel to fly the
temptations of Fascinia, recalls this warning just as he
is about to drink the magic draught, but even then is
unable to tear himself from the charming pleadings of
his temptress. As he wavers, Gabriel comes to stir

Arthur to nobler impulses, and Arthur, hurling down
the fatal bowl and paying no heed to Fascinia's laments,
follows the archangel back to the British hosts, having
successfully met all Satan's temptations and shown reason ultimately triumphant over the irrational.

This book is particularly rich in literary analogies.
First of all, it is noticeable that Blackmore begins the
temptation with a dragon fight which in its details
resembles the last exploit of the Red Cross Knight.
The description of the dragon is like Spenser's, even to
the three rows of teeth revealed by the gaping jaws. In
both stories the dragon is eventually overcome by his
enemy's thrusting his weapon down the dragon's throat.
Arthur's journey through the raging seas, the terrors of
the " Pictland Gulph," to which the terrors of Scylla
and Charybdis are nothing, and the dangerous area of
calm form a much simplified version of Guyon's trip to
the Bower of Bliss. The heaping up of terrors which
assail Arthur is analogous to the terrors of the
enchanted wood portrayed by Tasso, to the fairy storms
of the old romances and of Spenser, and to the daunt-
ing array of horrors assembled by Satan to terrify Christ
in *Paradise Regained*. The temptations of Fascinia bear
resemblance to Tasso, to Spenser, to Milton, and to
Dryden. In Tasso the knights seeking Rinaldo, who is
kept imprisoned by the charms of Armida, are enticed
by a table of dainty food, by music, by the argument
that it is fitting to indulge in pleasure as a rest from battle, and by passion. The languishing Rinaldo is stirred

to fly from Armida's charms by the two knights, but unlike Arthur, he again meets with Armida, and with reason in control, is able to withstand passion instead of resorting to flight. The visit of Arthur to Fascinia's castle strongly resembles Guyon's visit to the Bower of Bliss: the appeals to the senses through taste, through music, and through the physical beauty of Acrasia are the same appeals as are made to Arthur. Acrasia also has the powers of Circe and can change men into beasts. The use of the feast is reminiscent of the feast set before Christ by Satan in *Paradise Regained,* and the personal transportation of the one being tempted is also analogous. As has been previously pointed out, the temptation of Adam is the same as that offered in each of the above instances, the temptation of the irrational. Now in all these cases except in Blackmore the temptation is openly met, whatever the outcome; but in the case of Arthur and Fascinia, Arthur resorts to flight as he has been warned to do. Harington in his interpretation of the allegory of *Orlando Furiosa* suggests the advisability of this line of conduct: " in the fleshly conflicts and temptations, the only way to conquer is to play the coward and run away." He supports this idea by examples from both the romance and the Scriptures, saying:

Likewise in that Angelica flieth from Rinaldo, we may take an allegorical instruction, that the temptations of the flesh are overcome, chiefly by flying from them, as the Scripture it selfe teacheth, saying, Resist the divel, but fly fornication.

Thus it is that into the militant conception of virtue there creeps and intrudes and climbs the idea of safety through flight.

Though Blackmore makes few acknowledgments of the use of material from other writers, a heavy debt of literary influence is evident upon his pages. Like the bee, to which he is partial in his similes, he gathers from the choicest flowers of literature; he lacks, however, the power of distilling honey and in the end produces only wax.

Milton

Although Blackmore had not even mentioned Milton among the epic writers in his discussion of the epic, his use of Milton was so evident that in the Preface to *King Arthur* he had to admit that he had used " a few allusions to some Inventions of Milton, whom I look on as a very Extraordinary Genius." His true estimate of Milton is given in other writings. In his *Lay Monastery* he calls Milton " our great Milton " and says that his poem is " justly now acknowledg'd to be the most admirable Production of *British Genius*." He also praises Milton in his poem, *The Nature of Man,* and imitates his style and diction in his *Hymn to the Light of the World.* The Milton who gave Dryden only very grudging permission to " tag " his verses is not only freely plundered by Blackmore but also subjected to his praise. It is Milton's influence which has been noted by Maynadier, who says:

Taking a hint from *Paradise Lost,* he introduces two hostile bodies of supernatural beings, the fallen angels, who are

Arthur's enemies, and the angels of Heaven, who are Arthur's friends."

Havens points out that there is a debt to *Paradise Lost* in three of Blackmore's epics, the two Arthurian epics and *Eliza,* " since they employ Satan and his followers together with the archangels of heaven for their supernatural machinery." He naturally goes much further than Maynadier in his analysis of Milton's influence, points out the councils in hell as the " most Miltonic feature," lists some eight details which are drawn from Milton, and illustrates likenesses in diction. Oskar Liis in his thesis, *Die Arthurepen des Sir Richard Blackmore,* lists even the most minute and strained verbal parallels to Milton but does not even make a study of the larger points of similarity. Now the opposition between the hosts of Satan and of God may have been suggested by Milton; but Blackmore knew Tasso, who had already shown this conflict, depicted councils in hell, and portrayed a noble hero assailed by the arts of the devil and protected by the grace of heaven. It is likely, therefore, that Blackmore drew upon both sources in his portrayal.

As Blackmore points out in the Preface to *Prince Arthur,* his employment of Christian machinery in the place of the pagan gods used by Virgil or the Guardian Angels of the Kingdoms suggested by Dryden was in conscious and purposeful defiance of the critics who hold that

'tis scarce possible for a Christian Poet to make use of this advantage, of introducing Superior, Indivisible Powers into the

Action, and therefore seem to despair of seeing an Heroick Poem written now, that shall reach to the Dignity of those of the Pagans.

He undertook the *Prince Arthur,* he says, to give instance of his own belief that " our Theology may enter into an Epick Poem, and raise the Subject without being itself debas'd." In taking this stand, Blackmore was entering upon the discussion of an important critical topic of his age. Such poets as Vida, Tasso, and Du Bartas had won success in the use of Christian machinery, and the Christian epic had experienced an extensive vogue in France about the middle of the seventeenth century. French critics, however, had led the attack upon supernatural machinery in the Christian epic, arguing as Boileau expressed it:

> De la foi d'un chrétien les mystères terribles
> D'ornements égayés ne sont point susceptibles:
> L'Evangile à l'esprit n'offre de tous côtés
> Que pénitence à faire et tourments mérités;
> Et de vos fictions le mélange coupable
> Même à ses vérités donne l'air de la fable.

Le Moyne in the preface of *St. Louis* had contended against the employment of angels or demons on the ground that these spirits lessened the honor of the victory for mortals. Desmarets de Saint Sorlin had, however, argued that the "History of Christianity offered subjects far more inspiring to a poet than those which had been treated by Homer and Sophocles, and that

Christian poetry must bear off the palm from the pagan." The discussion in England had arisen in connection with Milton. Cowley held that "those mad stories of the *Gods* and *Heroes*" were used when "there was no other Religion, and therefore that was better than none at all," but Sir William Temple held that "true Religion" was inferior to "false" for fiction and that Christian machines "seemed rather to debase Religion than to heighten Poetry." One of the points on which Dennis criticized *Prince Arthur* was the use of angels and demons. The employment of angels, he states, is "contrary to the doctrine of the Church of England" for the reason that the "visible descent of an Angel must be a Miracle," and "Miracles had ceas'd a long time before *Prince Arthur* came into the World." Dennis goes on to explain why the machines in a Christian poem are not pleasing. Both angels and demons are so far removed from human nature that they have nothing in common with man, whereas the "Heathen Machines are enough out of Nature to be admirable and enough in Nature to delight." Milton's success in handling the fallen angels, he feels, is on account of the fact that Milton portrays the devils immediately after the fall when they still have some good in their natures, and he makes the change to entire evil a gradual one. Other poets cannot in the very nature of the case make a like portrayal and, according to Dennis, should not, therefore, undertake to use devils or to describe them. In the preface to the *Paraphrase of Job* Blackmore makes a heated attack upon the use of the " Rabble and Riffe raffe of Heathenish Gods " by a Christian poet, saying that there cannot be a more " intollerable Absurdity." In his *Essay upon Epick Poetry* Blackmore defends the use of Christian machinery at some length, advancing arguments to show that such supernatural aid to man enhanced the glory of religion and the importance of the hero. He illustrates by citing the use of God and Satan as opposing forces in *Job,* in Milton's epics, and in *Prince Arthur.* In all of these, he says, the " Dignity of Religion " has not been diminished. Later he adds to the argument, stating in the Preface to *Alfred* that since these supernatural powers are naturally in opposition, contention between them can be better handled. Blackmore also answers Boileau's objections to Christian machinery point by point, citing Dryden's opinion that an epic can be written upon " the Scheme of Revealed Religion." The conclusions of some of the other writers on this subject are very interesting. Davenant in his preface to *Gondibert* defends the Christian epic, though such men as Thomas Hobbes and Rymer are against it. Hobbes even goes so far as to say that it is no ornament to a poem " to profane the true God or invoke a false one."

Since *Paradise Lost* is the great example of the Christian epic in England, it is only natural to find Blackmore drawing heavily upon Milton. The result is a most incongruous melée of Geoffrey's history and *Paradise Lost,* a sort of a sequel, as it were, to the fall of man.

When *Prince Arthur* opens, Lucifer is still sulking over Christ's thwarting of his design in regard to man. Now that he has taken Albion for his " new conquer'd Seat," and he and his followers have set their altars there, it is especially distasteful to him to see the Christian Arthur approaching the shore. His ire is greatly aggravated by reminiscences of the war in heaven. In relating the story of the celestial struggle, Blackmore closely parallels Milton's account: the opposing forces are led by Lucifer and Michael; the wounds are not fatal on account of the " Aetherial mold " of the combatants; " massy Rocks of Heav'nly Chrystal flew," hurled by " the strong Arms of mighty Seraphs "; fire and thunder are used; Lucifer and Michael meet in single combat; Christ comes in a " Triumphant Chariot " and hurls the revolting forces into hell. Blackmore's Lucifer has something of the fine spirit of Milton's Satan. He boasts that he has set up a kingdom, though in hell, and that he has won fame by his fall; his is also the unconquerable spirit that will not yield. The use of Chaos and Old Night is similar to Milton's. When Lucifer is on his way to Lapland to get Thor to send a storm to wreck Arthur's fleet, Chaos and Old Night rejoice thinking that Nature, " would crack with universal Ruin " and their " lost Dominions " would be restored. Another and fuller picture of the Miltonic Chaos occurs in *King Arthur* where Satan gives the account of his flight through Chaos to the earth.

The office of many of the angels is the same as that

given by Milton. Uriel, for example, is used as the agent against Satan, and true to his Miltonic method of locomotion is "let by a golden Sunbeam thro' the Skies." In both *Prince Arthur* and *King Arthur,* Raphael, Adam's counsellor, is sent down to advise Arthur. Michael also continues the rôle of general, commanding the angelic hosts which guard Arthur. Gabriel in *King Arthur* protects Arthur during the period of temptation by Lucifer and finally rescues him from Lucifer's power, a mission which recalls the fact that Gabriel guards the gates of Eden and rescues man from the first attempts of Satan.

Whenever Lucifer is nonplused, he calls together an infernal council. Though such a device was common in the Christian epic, it is interesting to note that the councils described by Blackmore are much like the council in Pandemonium. Lucifer "in pride extended" generally presides from a golden throne. The speakers are briefly described and are of the same general character as Milton's speakers; their speeches are modeled after the same order and psychology.

Blackmore creates three figures after the conception of Sin pictured by Milton. The first is a Fury who has the power to stir man to passion and to give "present death" simply by breathing upon him. Even in her appearance she bears a mutilated likeness to Milton's figures of Sin and Death. In physical appearance she is as foul and revolting as Sin; like Death she is a vague shape:

No certain Shape, no Feature regular,
No limbs distinct in th' odious Fiend appear.

She inspires Lucifer with passion just as Sin new-sprung
from Satan's head inflamed her Sire:

The Prince of Darkness, leaping from his place,
Did in his Arms, his darling Fiend Embrace.

The next figure in this horrible trilogy is Discord,
bound to a rock at the edge of Chaos. One recalls
Hesiod's picture of Discord, but is even more impressed
by the likeness to Sin, in that monsters which " all each
other and their Parent tear " rage around her waist.
Like Sin, too, she had her birth in heaven at the time of
the disastrous revolt. The third monster dwells in the
midst of the enchanted wood. Her appearance is made
terrifying partly by its vagueness, for her form is black
and shapeless. The first two of these figures have an
effect upon nature similar to that of Sin. The Fury, con-
tracting " her vast dilate Size," flies through the night,
causing the spheres to stand amazed as they do when
sky rockets are set off! The analogy is much closer in
the case of Discord. When she comes to the castle of
Morogan, one of James's followers, nature feels the
effect of her presence. The " shrivel'd Fruit " drops
from " wither'd Boughs," and the flowers die:

Infection taints the Air, sick Nature fades
And suddain Autumn all the place invades.

The power to contract and expand in size; the ready
transformations; Satan's disguise as the " cherub strip-

ling "; the " thunder scars " and " faded splendor " of
the fallen angels—these are the kinds of details remind-
ing one of Milton and found recurring page after page.

It is not only in the passages devoted to supernatural
machinery, however, that Blackmore is dependent upon
Milton; there are also many parallels in other parts of
the story. The Saxons have about as many councils as
Lucifer, and these, too, follow the Pandemonium type.
Given the topic for the discussion at the meeting of the
council, one could almost reconstruct the order of the
addresses, the appeals of the speakers, the mob psychology. The three-day struggle of Arthur against Octa in
Prince Arthur is comparable to the three-day struggle
between God and Satan in heaven. On the first day the
combat is that of individual heroes; on the second day
there is a violent conflict under the leadership of the
great heads of the forces of good and evil; on the third
day Arthur is successful in overcoming the enemy
through his individual strength, as was Christ in the
heavenly combat. Blackmore is even thinking of Arthur
as Michael:

> As glorious *Michael,* when the Foe alarms
> The blissful Realms, clad in Celestial Arms,
> Bright as the Sun, leads forth th' Angelic Host
> To chase th' Invaders from the Heav'nly Coast,
> In such illustrious Arms the Prince was seen,
> His warlike Grace was such, and such his Godlike Mien.

Prince Arthur also contains the story of Eden,
recounted by Arthur to Hoel with Miltonic details.

Blackmore's conception of Adam and Eve is undoubtedly formed by Milton's. He almost copies Milton's
lines showing the inequality of the sexes:

> Of a more soft and nicely temper'd Mould,
> Her strokes were tender, his more strong and bold.
> Sweetness that ravish'd, milder than the Morn,
> And perfect Beauty did her Looks adorn.

Immediately there flashes through the mind:

> For contemplation he and valour formed,
> For softness she and sweet attractive grace.

The description of Eden contains the same type of portrayal of golden age condition that Milton gives.
Spring and autumn in harmonious union provide both
fruit and flowers. The earth brings forth without toil;
there is universal harmony, for neither man nor animal
preys upon other creatures and there is, therefore, no
fear. The beasts are all " mild and Tame "; the only
difference in the pictures is that Blackmore's lion pre-
fers to paw a bear instead of dandling the kid! The
deterioration in nature and in man which follows the
eating of the fruit, and the rise of the passions in man
are described by Blackmore with close adherence to the
account in *Paradise Lost* and in much the same lan-
gauge. Like Milton's, too, is Blackmore's conception
that when reason ceases to hold its place at the head of
the Scale of Nature, man becomes a prey to appetite:

> Reason dethron'd must the Commands obey
> Of this wild Rout, that holds the Sovereign sway.

The continued decadence of mankind is shown by both poets through the device of a vision of the future. As Uther shows to Arthur the succession of British rulers, the point is emphasized that one line of kings after another loses its original lustre and is superseded. This thought is additional to the portrayal of succession in either Virgil or Spenser.

It is not the purpose of this investigation to present the minor likenesses between Blackmore and Milton, the small details, the figures of speech, parallel passages, or vocabulary borrowings, for these may be found in Liis. That which interests us here is that Blackmore's extreme indebtedness to Milton is revealed not only in the mechanics of the epic—in the carrying out of his supernatural machinery where it might, by the very nature of the similarity be expected—but also in the philosophical thought.

Dryden

Blackmore's indebtedness is not only to the old masters of the epic, Virgil, Spenser, or even Milton, but in a peculiar manner also to a great contemporary poet. According to Dryden himself, Blackmore owed to Dryden the very suggestion of an Arthurian subject. In the preface to the translation of *Juvenal* Dryden, as was mentioned previously, set forth his idea of the use of the Guardian Angels of the Kingdoms for supernatural machinery in the epic, and suggested " king Arthur, conquering the Saxons " as a suitable subject in which

to incorporate the idea. Three years after Dryden's suggestion Blackmore published his first Arthurian epic.
In the Preface to the *Fables* Dryden accuses Blackmore
of taking over his plan, saying: " from that preface, he
plainly took his hint; for he began immediately upon
the story, though he had the baseness not to acknowledge his benefactor, but instead to traduce me in a
libel " (Blackmore's criticism of contemporary plays in
the Preface to *Prince Arthur*). Apparently Dryden felt
keenly Blackmore's failure to make acknowledgment
for the suggestion. In a letter to Dennis he had previously shown his touchiness in this respect, for he had
remarked concerning his plan for an Arthurian epic
that the probability was that no poet of his own day
would use the machinery he had devised " for fear of
discovering his own Ignorance; or if he should, he
might perhaps be ingrateful enough not to own me for
his Benefactor." Blackmore does not use the Guardian
Angels of the Kingdoms, which Dryden says sneeringly
were " machines too ponderous for him to manage,"
but it is very likely that Dryden started him upon the
subject and suggested the incorporation into this story of
the " opposition of ill spirits to good." Furthermore, in
his own defense of supernatural machinery in a Christian
poem Blackmore quotes Dryden's remarks upon the
same subject. There seems little doubt that Dryden was
justified in his point of view, for Blackmore also seems
to have employed certain details from Dryden's *King
Arthur* in his own story. The use of the beautiful Saxon

Princess as the prize for which Arthur fights against the Saxons is patently derived from Dryden, only the name is changed from Emmeline to Ethelina. The conception of Merlin is much the same as that held by Dryden. In both Dryden and Blackmore, Merlin is portrayed in the rôle of enchanter on the side of the Saxons. In no other literature that I have read is Merlin shown using his power against Arthur. Though undoubtedly Tasso is the original for the enchanted forest in both Dryden and Blackmore, there are noticeable parallels in the two pictures presented by the English authors. It is, however, in the temptation scene that the most striking likenesses occur. In Dryden, Arthur is on the point of succumbing to the enticements of his woman temptress, even though he knows that to do so is contrary to the dictates of reason, when Philidel intervenes; similarly in Blackmore, Arthur wavers before the temptation of Fascinia, but Gabriel comes to rescue him.

POLITICAL ALLEGORY

This general borrowing is, however, less significant than Blackmore's imitation of Dryden's application of ancient stories to contemporary events. In a broad way political allegory had been employed by the old poets. It had afforded primarily a means of flattering the ruler or depicting the outstanding events of a reign and had not been minutely applied. The allegorical treatment of large contemporary events and prominent characters had been used by Spenser; by the two writers of unpublished epics of the reign of Charles I, Samuel Sheppard in his *Faerie King* and Robert Jegon (?) in *A Supplement of the Faery Queene;* and by James Howell in his *Dodona's Grove; or the Vocal Forest,* in which some of the leading European events from 1603 to 1640 are given. But such exact and recognizable identification of persons and events in contemporary affairs as Blackmore used was something new in the field of the epic. It was found in the pastoral romance where, following the custom of the Hôtel de Rambouillet, prominent people were presented under the veil of certain romantic pseudonyms; from this type developed the society of the "matchless Orinda." It was used in pageants and masques, and employed by Jonson and Chapman in their plays. Satire from the time of Skelton had indulged in cipher, for without exact identification understood by contemporaries the satire would have lost its significance. Dryden in both satires and plays adapted old stories to portray contemporary events, definitely identifying events and characters. Since Blackmore's purpose in writing was also political and he drew his inspiration from Dryden, it seems very natural that he should adopt the type of political allegory which Dryden used. In the *Essay upon Epick Poetry* Blackmore designates this political allegory in the epic as an " agreeable " form in which the " chief Actors, especially the principal Hero, are made the Types of some illustrious Persons, whose Actions and Manners are shadow'd forth by the Qualities of those that act in the poem." He adds that " the

artful disguise should be drawn so thin that the real
Characters in the View and Intention of the Poet may
appear underneath, and be seen with ease through the
transparent Veil." Blackmore has identified more than
the chief characters with contemporary figures, but in
each case the disguise is so very light that identification
is readily made. As to the hero, the account of Arthur
taken from Geoffrey is made to exhibit the acquisition
of the British throne by the Prince of Orange, as has
been pointed out by both Maynadier and W. Lewis
Jones. To the political allegory is due a number of
changes which Blackmore makes in Geoffrey's story. It
is necessary for Blackmore to get Arthur to Holland; so
he represents the young prince as being sent to the court
of Odar after the death of Uther. Arthur is brought up
there, developing the traits by which the Prince of
Orange is popularly known—love of the hunt in times
of peace and a courage in battle which takes him to the
head of the forces. He wins fame for himself in the
Netherlands by his warfare with the Gauls and attracts
" British knights opprest at home." In this section one
almost loses sight of the fact that the name used is
Arthur, so closely do the facts coincide with history.
Finally, Arthur is invited by ten nobles to rescue England
from the Saxons, an obvious use of the petition brought
to the Prince of Orange by Herbert and other nobles.
The storm which shipwrecks Arthur on the coast of
Armorica is based upon the fact that the Prince of
Orange was delayed by storms and unfavorable winds

when he attempted to go to England. The naval battle before the landing of Arthur is not, or course, historical, for the fleet of James did not attack the Prince of Orange but merely hemmed him in after he reached the harbor. The victory of Arthur by sea is evidently inserted to elevate the prowess of the hero. Arthur, like the Prince of Orange, lands in the west and makes a triumphant march to London, being joined on the way by the leading nobles. Unlike the Prince, however, he engages in many bloody battles and does great deeds with his famous sword, Caliburno. In the Saxon Council (comparable to the Council held in London by James) Pascentius (Danby) advises the chief of the Saxons to try to reach a peaceful settlement with Arthur by offering him his Christian daughter, Ethelina, in marriage. One sees in this overture a representation of the alliance between the Protestant Princess Mary, the daughter of James II, and the Prince of Orange. After his conquest of England, Arthur is shown continuing his campaign in Ireland and Scotland before he is crowned. The campaign against Tyrconnel with the sickness and death in the camp of Schomberg is clearly portrayed in Blackmore's account of Megaera's coming from hell with disease and visiting the camp with death. The Scottish campaign in Blackmore is a queer mixture of various events from Geoffrey. The Scottish chief, Tollo, who comes with Macbeth, Mordred, and others to the aid of the Saxons, becomes Geoffrey's Flollo of the siege of Paris. The single combat between Arthur and Tollo

follows the details related by Geoffrey in his account of
the meeting of Arthur and Flollo. The whole incident,
however, is meant to represent the campaign of the
Prince of Orange against Dundee.

The political allegory in *King Arthur* is even more
obvious and far less complex. After gaining the English crown, King William joins in the continental struggle against Louis XIV. This event is depicted from
Geoffrey as Arthur's conquest of Lutetia or Paris. William is recalled to England by the plots instigated by
Louis XIV to restore James to the throne in his absence.
An uprising by Mordred, as in Geoffrey, thinly veils the
contemporary history. William quells this rebellion,
returns to the continent, and escapes a conspiracy to take
his life as he goes about among the army posts. In giving this account, Blackmore uses the very thrilling tale
of the conspiracy of the Saxons to betray the British
forces and take the life of Arthur. Finally Namur is
taken, and the peace of Ryswick follows in 1697; these
events are shown as the fall of Lutetia and the victorious
conquest by Arthur.

RELIGIOUS ALLEGORY

The above account of Blackmore's use of the Arthurian matter found in Geoffrey is only the dullest part of
the story. The additions which he makes to this material stir one's curiosity and finally real interest. To provide supernatural machinery for his epic, Blackmore uses
the old contest between God and Satan, putting God,

Michael, Gabriel, Raphael, Uriel, and the heavenly hosts on the side of Arthur, and Lucifer and his followers on the side of the Saxons. It is an obvious conclusion from the text that Blackmore is incorporating the religious struggle between Protestants and Catholics which gave particular significance to the Revolution in England. As Arthur, the Christian Worthy, William is the champion of the Protestant faith against the " pagan " Catholics. Macaulay testifies that this idea was in keeping with the belief of the time, which saw in William a man set apart as Samson had been " to be the champion of all free nations and all pure Churches." After Dennis changes his support to the House of Orange, he writes of William as the " Protector of Liberty and Religion," the " Great Soul that watch'd the Christian World." The first work of William, as the first work of Elizabeth had been, was the restoration of Protestantism, and it is only natural that Blackmore, following Spenser, should depict in allegory this conflict of Protestantism with Catholicism.

According to Blackmore, Satan and his followers (Catholicism) have set up pagan altars in England during the reign of the Saxon chief, Octa (James II). England is suffering from this pagan oppression (the persecution of Protestants under James) and calls upon the Christian Prince Arthur to free her:

> His Arms the lowring Tempest shall dispel,
> That threat'ning Albion, rolls from Rome and Hell.
> Fair Liberty her drooping Head shall rear,
> And blest Religion on her Throne appear.

Satan fears that he and his followers shall be routed from their English domains and tries to prevent the coming of Arthur by the storm previously mentioned; but Uriel, sent by God to rescue Arthur, stills the waves with his heavenly lyre. God gives further aid by sending a vision to the Armorican Hoel and by commanding Raphael to visit the praying Arthur and to reveal to him the entire biblical cycle from the creation to the judgment, the story with which Arthur is to complete the conversion of Hoel and win his assistance. God again sends Raphael to Arthur's aid when Satan commissions a fury to waste the camp with disease. In all battles Michael and the heavenly hosts encompass Arthur, and Satan and his followers assemble to protect the Saxons. In the end the Christian daughter of the pagan chief, won by Arthur in marriage, is, as we have seen, the Protestant daughter of the Catholic James. By God's favor the Protestants attain an ultimate victory in England and establish a Protestant king.

King Arthur continues the story of the conflict between the Protestants and the Catholics by portraying William's part in relieving the suffering Protestants on the continent from the Catholic oppressions of Louis XIV. Satan sends Discord, disguised as a Catholic Churchman, to some of the loyal Catholics in England and is responsible for the plot to restore James II to the throne while Arthur (William) is on the continent, an incident similar in its details to Milton's portrayal of the Catholic plot in *In Quintum Novembris*. God, on the other hand, enables Arthur to overcome the work of Discord, supports him by granting him the companionship of Gabriel when he is subjected to Satan's direct power, and finally aids him in winning a magnificent victory over the Catholics, who are supported by Satan. Not only is the story of King Arthur forced into the mold of contemporary political and religious events, or the characters given the distinguishing traits of historical personages, but even the names used frequently leave no doubt as to the person intended. It would have been a dull nation indeed that could fail to identify, for example, such names as Trelon for Trelawney, Hebar for Herbert, Solmar for Solms, Sakil for Sackville, Galbut for Talbot, or Shobar for Schomberg.

That this political and religious significance was intended by Blackmore and not just extracted afterwards at leisure, according to the recipe of Martinus Scriblerus, is proved by the extant interpretation of some of his contemporaries. *An Epistle to Sir Richard Blackmore* was written after the battle of Blenheim, pleading with him to celebrate the victories of Marlborough. In this it is shown that Arthur was publicly recognized as William by Blackmore's contemporaries:

> Or dos't thou still for the *Great* WILLIAM grieve,
> Tho' he will *ever* in thy *Arthur* live?
> Or, is *One Poet* to *One Heroe* due,
> T'AUGUSTUS *Virgil,* and to WILLIAM *you?*

When Blackmore replied with a sketch for an epic on Marlborough, he further revealed his bent for showing contemporary characters and events under the cover of allegory by suggesting that the poets give an " allegoric view " of Marlborough by using Constantine. Indeed, the use of old stories to veil the political significance of his poems is practiced by Blackmore in all his epics. His *Eliza* gives support to Anne, " a new Eliza," under the cover of the story of Queen Elizabeth, and his *Alfred,* dedicated to Prince Frederick of Hanover, is for the aid of the new sovereign. In the preface to *Alfred* he clearly states his own political and religious intent when he says:

I had the Honour to contribute more to the Succession of the illustrious House of *Hanover* to the Crown of *Great-Britain,* than I ever boasted of, contenting my Self with this, that what I had done was for the Service of reformed Religion, and the Good of my Country.

He considers the reigning monarch " A Christian, not a *Pagan* " since he is Protestant and recommends to the Prince the study of the way in which he has " stemm'd the violent Tide of Party-Fury," kept down rebellion, saved the country from " Popish Tyranny, from corrupt and deformed Christianity, from the sad Restoration of our former Calamities, and the terrible Treatment of an enraged Pretender." In Dennis's criticism, *Remarks on Prince Arthur,* 1696, we definitely learn that *Prince Arthur* was considered to be designed for the service of both state and church. Dennis has to defend himself in his introduction against those who object to his book on the ground " that it was intended

to expose a Poem which was design'd for the service of
the Government." He says that this objection "was
urg'd with all the force, that it was capable of receiving. That the Government comprehended the Church
and State, for both which I had in a peculiar manner
declar'd; and therefore to invalidate that which was
design'd for the Service of both, would show alteration
of Mind or want of Thought." He says, also, that if the
state is concerned "there must be a parallel between the
late Revolution and the Expedition of Arthur" and
admits that it is affirmed that "Prince Arthur was
designed to resemble the King." Though Dennis himself takes the matter rather lightly, he reveals that there
were men "who look'd upon the Writing against Prince
Arthur as the committing a Crime of State, and the
incurring a premunire." We learn, furthermore, that
some of the clergy went so far as "violently to
espouse" *Prince Arthur*. In February of the year following the publication of *Prince Arthur* Blackmore was
knighted, and this honor was attributed by the Wits to
his book. Now William was not such a patron of literature as to confer this honor lightly for literary efforts
alone, and it seems likely that it was Blackmore's political service that gave him his rank. In regard to *King
Arthur* Blackmore himself says, "the Judicious Reader
will soon find in the Poem it selfe, the true Reason why
I could keep it no longer by me." The material used was
later published in a prose tract entitled *A true and
impartial History of the Conspiracy against King William of glorious memory in the year 1695."*

The publication of *King Arthur* brought forth another critical attack indicating the political and religious basis for discrediting the work of Blackmore. The anonymous author of *Homer and Virgil not to be compar'd with the two Arthurs* adopts the form of a letter to a friend for his criticism. According to the introductory paragraph, the friend had commanded the critic to read these poems and give his opinion of them, and had given the critic " very important Reasons " which had " forc't " him to make the request. As had Dennis in the criticism of *Prince Arthur,* this critic and his publisher attack the portrayal of the king and the clergy and make a thrust which must have really wounded Blackmore when they say that the representation of the clergy is worse than that in the Restoration plays which Blackmore so heartily detested. The gentleman who had concerned himself to get the opinion of these poems, which he termed " the most vicious and absurd Poetry that ever came from the Sons of Apollo," took the communication to Luke Meredith, a very reputable publisher, and again gave " important Reasons," this time for getting the manuscript published.

It is undoubtedly this political significance which caused the immediate popularity of *Prince Arthur.* There were two editions in 1695, one of ten books and one of twelve; another folio edition in 1696; and a third edition in 1714. Also, in 1700 Book I was translated into Latin by H. Hogaeus. It was praised by people of many classes. Men of such eminence as Molyneux and Locke spoke highly of it. Indeed, Molyneux goes to the extreme of saying that " all our English poets (except Milton) have been ballad makers in comparison to him." Locke was milder, though he says that Blackmore has " an extraordinary talent in poetry." Cotton Mather in *The Christian Philosopher* calls him " the incomparable Sir Richard Blackmore." Aaron Hill thought so much of *Prince Arthur* that he gave it to his little daughter to read! It even penetrated its way to a desolate inn in southern Scotland, where it and the Bible were the only two books found by Dr. Alexander Carlyle almost half a century later. The landlord said that *Prince Arthur* would divert Dr. Carlyle, and Dr. Carlyle remarks, " and so it did, for I had not met with it before."

Primarily because of his defense of the Revolution and the attack upon Catholicism Blackmore brought down upon himself an almost unprecedented storm of criticism, especially from the writers who had supported the Stuarts and Catholics. In writing his account of Blackmore, Anderson says, " hardly any writer has ever been more ridiculed than Blackmore." Here was an obscure physician who had suddenly turned man of letters, standing alone in opposition to the critical group of Covent Garden and flaunting in their faces his condemnation of the manner of writing adopted in the " late loose times," who had been knighted by the king and approved by the church. Swift makes reference to the fact that it is only upon " her seminaries of Gresham

and Covent Garden " that Criticism " lets fall her blessing," but Blackmore boasts that he has not sought their
favor or kissed the hands of " their Governour," by
whom, of course, he means Dryden, though he realizes
it is the custom of the writers of the day " who by
Assisting, Crying up, Excusing and Complementing one
another, carry on their Poetical Trade in a Joynt-
stock." Yet, says Blackmore, this group was unable to
ruin him and their criticism even helped him, " For their
Character and Temper, as well as the Grounds and Reasons of their Outcrys and Opposition were so well
known, that they could by no means pass for unbyas'd
and Disinterested Judges." The poet thinks that
although the critics pretended to be displeased with the
faults found in *Prince Arthur,* they " would have been
more displeas'd, if they had discover'd fewer."

The ridicule of Blackmore took many forms. Every
possible ground of criticism, and there were many
counts on which Blackmore was open to criticism, was
brought against him. Dryden led in the attack, embit-
tered by Blackmore's remarks upon contemporary drama
and his use without acknowledgment of Dryden's suggestion for a heroic poem: " It was not for this noble
knight," says Dryden, " that I drew the plan of an epic
poem on King Arthur." Dryden also frankly attributed
Blackmore's animosity to *Absalom and Achitophel,*
" which he (Blackmore) thinks is a little hard on his
fanatic patrons in London." By this remark he confirms
the political and religious source of the critical battle

which was waged over the Arthurian epics. In that day of the " Wits " no worse insult could be offered a work than to call it *dull,* and this epithet, often richly deserved, was applied constantly to Blackmore. Dryden cuts at Blackmore by calling him Maurus and at his work by saying, " Nothing ill is to be spoken of the dead; and, therefore, peace be to the Manes of his ' Arthurs.' " Since the physician professed to compose his epics as he drove to call on his patients, Dryden ridiculed his style by saying he " Writes to the rumbling of his coach's wheels." Blackmore retaliated in his *Satire on Wit,* which Dr. Johnson terms " a proclamation of defiance which united the poets almost all against him, and which brought upon him lampoons and ridicule from every side." Following this there was published a collection of lampoons called *Discommendatory Verses on those which are Truly Commendatory on the Author of the Two Arthurs and the Satyr against Wit.* Swift, Garth, Sedley, and Pope were among the prominent writers in addition to Dryden who poured scorn upon the physician-epic-poet. They made fun of his degrees, his method of composition, pomposity of verse, and ceaseless productivity. Stirred by Pope's burlesque of a Psalm, Blackmore accused Pope of " profaneness and immorality," in return for which Pope heaped ridicule upon him and made him immortal in the *Dunciad* as the " everlasting Blackmore " who " sings so loudly and who sings so long." He calls Blackmore " the father of the Bathos, and indeed the Homer of it," and

Swift in *Martinus Scriblerus* compiled all his best examples of Bathos from Blackmore. In the *Battle of the Books* Swift has Lucan present Blackmore with spurs and represents him as protected by the goddess Dulness. The criticism of Blackmore became so widespread that it had point in a contemporary comedy, *Love's Last Shift,* in which Narcissa says that the criticism of her lover "has much the same effect as the coffee-critics ridiculing *Prince Arthur;* for I have found a pleasing disappointment in my reading you."

Blackmore seemed little disconcerted by all the abuse poured out upon him and in the preface to the *Paraphrase of Job* stated, "If I can escape the Defamation of their Panegyricks, I think myself very safe."

The attempt to laugh Blackmore out of countenance was not the only effort made to discredit and silence him. A short time after the appearance of *Prince Arthur* John Dennis produced his critical volume, *Remarks upon Prince Arthur,* which is said to have brought Blackmore into celebrity, an effect opposite to that intended. It is only natural that Dennis should have concerned himself in the attack upon Blackmore, for he was Dryden's friend and at the time still loyal to the Stuarts. Pope says that King William's knighting Blackmore also incensed Dennis, making " surly Dennis swear." Since Blackmore had taken over Bossu's definition of the epic in his Preface to *Prince Arthur* and had emphasized the idea that the great epic writers were made by following the rules, Dennis undertook to show

that Blackmore neither understood the nature of an epic
nor obeyed the critical tenets. He advances amusing and
ingenious proof that Blackmore did not even write an
epic. He divides the fable into two parts, the truth or
moral "which is its foundation," and the action which
conveys this moral. He then states that some of Blackmore's episodes contradict his moral; hence the foundation is destroyed. Since there can be no fable without a
foundation, therefore there is no epic! He also under-
takes to show that the action is not " one and entire,"
and that the narration is " neither probable, delightful,
nor wonderful." Though instruction may be the chief
end of the poet, Dennis holds that " Diversion is the
principal Aim of the Reader " as well as an aid to
instruction, and goes on to show that Blackmore fails
to please because he has too few incidents, these are
not in their nature agreeable, there is no variety in
either content or style, and his incidents are neither
pathetic, nor since they are drawn from Virgil, surpris-
ing. Dennis devotes some time to refuting the idea that
Prince Arthur is a work of importance to the state and
church. He picks flaws with the representation of William as Arthur, holding that Arthur experiences fear
and is concerned for himself more than for his subjects, qualities which would make a " more unjust and
a more unreasonable Character of him than his most
Malicious and most Profligate Enemies have been
known to invent." As for the church, he says this epic
could not possibly be of service but should rather be

censured than supported by the clergy, since its supernatural machines required the violation of the very doctrines of the church. Dr. Johnson in his life of Blackmore calls the criticism of Dennis " more tedious and
disgusting than the work which he condemns." Blackmore in the Preface to *King Arthur* admits some faults
of construction in his work, and he holds no lasting
resentment towards Dennis. In his Preface to *Alfred* he
calls Dennis " superior in critical ability to Mr. Boileau." This tribute may, however, refer to Dennis's
praise of *The Creation!* Furthermore, after Anne's
accession, Dennis had written in support of the Revolution and had won favor with the queen and court. The
Duke of Marlborough had become sufficiently interested in him to recommend him as a royal waiter in the
port of London, and he and Blackmore were no longer
political enemies.

A second formal critical attack was made upon Blackmore in 1700. This is an anonymous book entitled
*Homer and Virgil not to be compar'd with the Two
Arthurs,* to which reference has previously been made.
In the *Terms Catalogue* where this volume is listed,
the two Arthurs are parenthetically given as " by J.
Dryden and Sir R. Blackmore," and the book is assumed
to be written by Blackmore. These assumptions are,
however, not correct. The two Arthurs are the *Prince
Arthur* and the *King Arthur* of Blackmore and the
title of the work is satiric. The purpose of the little
volume is to discredit Blackmore. Even the letter from

" The Publisher to the Reader " follows the satirical tone of the author. It is probably to this critical work that the author of the parody on *Advice to the Poets* refers when he says:

The Ghosts of Homer and Virgil are resolv'd to see if there are more Faults in your Writings, than you pretend to have found in theirs.

The text of the volume begins with a table of passages from *Prince Arthur, King Arthur,* and the *Paraphrase of Job,* the purpose of which seems to be to show instances of Blackmore's repetition and to make him seem as trivial and ridiculous as possible. *Miscellany Collections* from the poems follow. The critic likens them to " a Bundle of useless, prickly, and ill-scented Weeds." The criticism proper begins with the sarcastic ridicule of separate lines, more ridiculous in itself in the straining for satire than the passages which it should discredit. Among other charges the critic attributes Blackmore's poetic productivity to the desire " to procure a Reputation in Medicine," and holds up the dangers of the poet-physician to the patient. What will be the outcome, he inquires, if " a fit of Versifying " comes on " when the *Paroxysm* in a double *Tertian* may be rising with greater Fury." When the more serious criticism is reached, the anonymous writer begins as Dennis with Bossu's definition of the epic and after recommending Dennis's treatment of *Prince Arthur,* says that he will follow the method used by Dennis and treat of *King Arthur.* Especial grounds for criticism are lack of action

on the part of the hero, long set speeches at inappro-
priate times, the extended descriptions of the king's followers, the diction, which is not comparable to Homer
and Virgil, and such matters. The ancients and the
moderns are then compared with especial discredit to
Blackmore. The tedious critic is far less amusing than
Blackmore himself and only occasionally shows the
penetration revealed in the remark that these are
" poems without poetry."

It has been said that the deluge of criticism of Blackmore was followed by a loss of practice as a physician,
but Anderson thinks this claim doubtful and cites some
communications in the *Gentlemen's Magazine* for 1792
showing that " persons of the highest rank " sought
him out and he " preserved his professional credit and
reputation till the close of his life."

The study of Blackmore's epics and their political and
religious significance brings us to the close of the century. There are few more fascinating stories in the history of literature than that of the vicissitudes of the
Arthurian legend, and this seventeenth century chapter
of that story is of peculiar interest and importance. It
has revealed to us a poetic legend shorn of its romance
and used by statesmen for the practical purpose of politics; it has accounted for the discredit heaped upon this
British legend with the development of interest in law
and the new admiration for the Saxons; it has shown
how it fell into a period of extreme disrepute with the
downfall of the Stuarts and the establishment of the

Commonwealth; and it has indicated the substitution for the traditional British-Tudor-Stuart usage by a new kind of employment growing out of the changed conception of political allegory which in the later years of the century implied the use of parallel ancient stories for the discussion of contemporary people and events. It remains for some eighteenth century scholar to show the relation of this legend to the medieval revival and to indicate the way in which romance and mysticism, the loves of knights and ladies, and the search for the Holy Grail, again supersede the cold arguments for the reality of Arthur's existence and the grim accounts of his exploits in battle.

COMMENTARY AND BIBLIOGRAPHICAL NOTES

FOR CHAPTER I

Page 1. The use of Arthurian-British material in support of the Tudor claims to the throne is fully discussed by Professor Edwin Greenlaw in his *Studies in Spenser's Historical Allegory.* Certain points are also brought out by A. E. Parsons in " The Trojan Legend in England," in *MLR,* July and October, 1929, and by C. B. Millican in " Spenser and the Arthurian Legend," in *RES,* April, 1930.

Page 4. The reference is to *The Beginning of the History of Great Britain, Works,* ed. Spedding, VI. 277. The account of conditions preceding the death of Elizabeth and at the accession of James is the clearest analysis of the complex situation that I have been able to find. Bacon points out that the people had grown weary of the long reign of Elizabeth and that the natural law of change was operative, as well as the desire to be free from the whims of a capricious woman and the too-strict insistence upon prerogative. That disaster did not follow upon the accession of James, he attributes also to the unquestionable rights of James, to the relief from uncertainty concerning the future—it was " as a man that awaketh out of a fearful dream "—, and to the great desire for union. He also refers to the personal hopes of various groups in the kingdom. The followers of Essex, who had been in danger of their lives, once more felt secure; both Puritans and Papists were hopeful of favor; and the nobility rejoiced in renewed security.

Camden in *Annals of Queen Elizabeth* also gives an interesting account of this period. The quotation is from the fourth edition, London, 1668, p. 660. In the account of the *Entertainment of 1603* Dekker gives amusing expression to the change from fear to sudden joy among the people at the proclamation of the succession of James:

The feared wounds of a civill sword . . . being stopt from bursting foorth, by the sound of Trompets that proclaimed King *Iames*: All mens eyes were presently turned to the North, standing even stone-stil in their Circles, like the poynts of so many Geometricall needles, through a fixed and Adamantine desire to behold this 45. yeares wonder.

Page 5. Parsons in "The Trojan Legend in England," in *MLR*, October, 1929, discusses more fully the identification of James with the infant crowned in his cradle, and tells of the great desire for unity expressed in the literature of even the fifteenth and sixteenth centuries and the prevalent belief that through Brute and Arthur, England had a right to claim not only Scotland but also France.

Page 6. Joy over the proclaimed union was expressed in many of the speeches of welcome made to James. Samuel Daniel in "A Panegyric Congratulatory, delivered to the King's Most Excellent Majesty, at Burly-Harington" (Nichols, *Progresses of James I*, I. 133) calls the union a conspiracy of Time, Fate, and Fortune, and rejoices that

> No Scot, no English now, nor no debate.
> What heretofore could never yet be wrought
> By all the swords of power, by blood, by fire,
> By ruin and destruction: here's brought to pass
> With peace, with love, with joy, desire.

John Savile at Theobalds (*Salutatory Poem to King James*, 1603, in Nichols, I. 143) calls for thanksgiving over this union which was effected for the first time since the days of Brutus. Chettle sings a paean of joy over the quenching of the "heat of wrath and boiling blood" by this "blessed unity" (*Shepherd's Spring Song for James*, in *Harl. Misc.*, II. 506). Campion feels that now "old debate to love and kindness turns" (*Masque at Lord Hay's Marriage*, 1606-7, in Nichols, II. 121). Robert Glover (*English Genealogy*, London, 1610, " To the learned and modest Reader ") rejoices that " after so long distraction " the nation is united " in One Happinesse, vnder One true-God, One true-Religion, and One true-King and Monarch of Great-Brittaine (King James)." Even foreign nations shared this joy with England, and in France John Gordon dedicated to James "A Panegyric of Congratulation for the Concord of the Realmes of Great Britaine in Vnitie of Religion and vnder one King." This was translated into English in the year of the accession by E. Grinston. Later poets also celebrated the welding of the nations under one king: Beaumont in *Bosworth Field,* Slatyer in *Palae-Albion,* and even Patrick Hannay, who writes of the mission of James in warming " the frozen-love betwixt the *Tay* and *Thames* " (*Elegie* II).

This proclamation by James is given in Robert Steele's *Tudor and Stuart Proclamations,* Oxford, MCMX, I. no. 1002. See also Prothero, G. W., *Statutes and Constitutional Documents,* 1558-1625 (4th ed., Oxford, 1913), p. 393.

Page 7. The prophecy given by Geoffrey is in *The History of Britain,* ed. J. A. Giles (Bohn Edition) in *Six Old English Chronicles,* p. 199.

The quotation from Bacon is found in *Works,* ed. Spedding, VI. 275.

Page 10. The anagram cited is referred to in the edition of 1870, p. 185. It appeared in 1595 in a work by Walter Quin written for James in reply to what was considered a derogatory protrayal of Mary, Queen of Scots, in Spenser's *Faerie Queene.* Four *anagrammata in nomen Jacobi sexti* in four languages were included. See Evelyn Albright's *Dramatic Publication in England, 1580-1640,* New York, 1927, p. 151.

Page 11. The quotation in regard to King James's avowed imitation of King Arthur is taken from the letter of the Venetian State Secretary, *Calendar Venetian State Papers,*

1603-7, no. 106. These papers throw much interesting light upon the entire period.

Page 12. The full account of the entertainment is found in Thomas Dekker's *The Whole Magnificent Entertainment Given to King James . . . the 15 of March, 1603*, London, 1614. This is a rare book but is to be found in the Elizabethan Club of Yale University. The account of the Italians' pageant to which reference is here made occurs on the page opposite C_3. A somewhat less complete report is given in Nichols, *Progresses James I*, I.

Page 13. The description of the Arch of Triumph above the Conduit on Fleet Street is found in both sources, Dekker, p. (H_4) and Nichols, I. 370.

This age was to be not only an age of peace but also a period in which righteousness and judgment prevailed. These ideas were stressed again and again in the speeches of welcome to the king (*Ibid.*, I. 133, 275, 332). They were also used in the *Entertainment of the Two Kings of Great Britain and Denmark at Theobalds*, July 24, 1606 (*Ibid.*, II. 70). The Fleet Street Arch at the time of the entry of James into London represented Justitia, Fortitudo, Temperantia, and Prudentia opposite England, Scotland, France, and Ireland. Richard Martin in his *Speech to the King at Stamford Hill*, 1603 (*Ibid.*, I. 130) remarked that Scotland had tried the king's prudence, "Ireland shall require your justice . . . France shall prove your fortitude . . . but let England be the schoole, wherein your Majestie will practice your temperance and moderation."

Wilson's *History of the Reign of James I* (1653) is found in White Kennett's *Complete History of England*, London, 1719, II. The reference is to p. 661. Roger Coke is the author of the *Detection of the Court and State of James I*. The reference is found I. 33 (1719).

Page 14. The description of the Arch of Triumph at Temple-Bar is from Nichols, I. 390-91.

Page 18. The Latin text of this dialogue was bound up with Dr. Matthew Gwynne's *Vertumnus* and is quoted by Furness, *A New Variorum: Macbeth,* and in part in *Progresses James I,* I. 543, by Brydges, *Censura Literaria,* II. 74, and by Parsons, *op. cit.,* Oct., 1929. Farmer in his *Essay on the Learning of Shakespeare* (London, 1767, p. 56) also quotes from *Rex Platonicus.* See *Rex Platonicus,* Oxford, 1635, pp. 29 ff. Miss Winstanley in the introduction to *Hamlet and the Scottish Succession* explains Shakespeare's choice of the subject of *Macbeth* as a compliment to King James. It is for this reason, she says, that prophecy is stressed, Macbeth dwells on succession, the future is revealed to show the line of Fleance succeeding to the throne, and the unity of the kingdom is portrayed in the " two-fold balls and treble sceptres."

Page 20. *The Triumphes of Re-United Britain* is given in full in Nichols, I. 564 ff.

Page 23. The letter to Sir Thomas Campbell is quoted in Nichols II. 320.

FOR CHAPTER II

Page 28. The proclamation suppressing Cowell's *Interpreter* is quoted in Albright's *Dramatic Publication in England,* 1580-1640, p. 82, from Steele's *Proclamations,* no. 1092. F. W. Maitland's splendid essay on *English Law and the Renaissance* (London, 1901) not only gives an historical sketch of the development of law during this period but also throws much light upon the political life of the succeeding century and suggests lines for further study.

Page 29. Selden restates these ideas very pithily in his *Table Talk:* "All is as the state pleases " (p. 28) ; " every law is a contract between the king and the people, and therefore to be kept " (p. 65) ; " to know what Obedience is due to the Prince, you must look into the Contract betwixt him and his people . . . When the Contract is broken . . . then the Decision is by Arms " (p. 115). The references are to the edition by Edward Arber, London, 1869.

Page 31. The reference to *A Review Appended to the History of Tythes* is found in Selden's *Works*, ed. David Wilkins, London, 1724, III. part 2, col. 1333. On this point see also W. W. Lucas, *The Corporate Nature of English Sovereignty*, London, 1911.

Page 32. The reference is to *Catalogus Librorum Manuscriptorum Bibliothecae Cottonianae*, by Thomas Smith, Oxford, 1696.

Page 33. The summons before the Court of High Commission is discussed by J. S. Burns in his *Court of High Commission*, London, 1865, p. 37.

Page 35. The quotation is from *A Courtier's Censure of the King's Intertaynment at Both Universities*, in Nichols, *op. cit.*, III. 74. *Ignoramus*, written by George Ruggle, was entered in the Stationers' Register, 18 April, 1615: *Ignoramus: Comoedia prout Cantabrigiae acta fuit coram Jacobo sereniss potentiis. Magnae Britaniae Rege."* The play was not published, however, until 1630 and then not from the author's manuscript, which seems to have been destroyed. I am using the 3rd edition, London, 1658. In the *Encomiasticon in Ignoramum* the author suggests the content of the play:

> Hic sunt statuta Regis; hic est Iustinianus;
> Solicitorum greges; Attorney rusticanus;
> Pandectas tibi Iuris, (et) Chartam Magnam dabo,
> Cum Tabulis duodecem, (et) totas in octavo.

The account of the king's enjoyment of the play is in Hawkins's edition of *Ignoramus* and is quoted by Nichols, *op. cit.*, III. 87.

Page 37. The story of this severity even toward students is found in G. P. Gooch, *The History of English Democratic Ideas in the Seventeenth Century*, Cambridge, 1898, p. 68, note 6.

Page 38. The protest of Parliament is quoted from the *Journal of the House of Commons* by von Raumer in his *Political History of England*, London, 1837, I. 443.

The pageant of 1620 was Squire's *Triumphs of Peace*. The description of the Iron Age is an interesting one: in a chariot was Time, " seated upon an houre-glasse that was supported on the shoulders of a gyant representing the Iron Age "; Time calls the Iron Age the last prop of the world and says that if he were gone, the elements, which were his attendants in the chariot, " would with rage turne feeble Time to desolation." See Nichols, *op. cit.*, IV. 624.

Page 39. The information in regard to Coke's library is taken from C. W. James, *Chief Justice Coke*, London, 1929, p. 312. This is a delightful book giving much valuable information in regard to the manner of living both in London and on the great estates as well as throwing light upon the affairs of state. Mr. James was for years librarian of the Earl of Leicester, in whose great library at Holkam family documents and many other manuscripts as well as rare books are treasured. He has had an opportunity, therefore, to gain an unusually intimate knowledge of the family about which he has written. Many private papers have been accessible to him, and the details concerning travel and household affairs which he drew from the account books of the sixteenth and seventeenth centuries are especially interesting for the light which they throw upon the social life of the period.

Page 40. Powell's discussion is in his *The Antiquity, Authority and Uses of Lèets*, London, 1641, p. 19. The reference from Spelman is in the *Reliquiae Spelmannianae*, Oxford, London, 1698, p. 100.

Page 41. The quotation denoting the change in the conception of history is from *State Tracts*, 1660-87, London, 1692, *Preface to the Reader*.

Page 42. This summary from L'Isle is taken from his

Anglo-Saxon Treatise, London, 1623, *To the Reader,* Sections 11, 12, 16. Sir John Spelman's *Saxon-English Psalter* was published " to preserve the memory of our mother chvrche and language, and to further the studye of our antiquityes and lawes."

Page 44. The reference to Bacon is to *The Advancement of Learning,* ed. James Edward Creighton, New York, 1900, p. 51; that to Selden, *History of Tythes* (" Dedication to Sir Robert Cotton "), *Works,* III. part ii; that to Milton's *History,* p. 203 of the 1677 edition.

Page 46. Spelman's account, taken from the *Glossary,* "Authoris de se et Opera sua, Praefatio " is as follows:

Libros et arma literaria . . . undequaque comparo, accinctusque jam in hanc militiam, Patres, Concilia, medii seculi Authores, et qui ad rem antiquam pertinent tam extraneam quam domesticam, sedulus volvo et evolvo. Occurrunt passim peregrini labii vocabula: Gothici, Vandalici, Saxonici, Germannici, Longobardici, Normannici, etc. ignotae functionis ministeria, Officia, dignitates, Magistratus, et infinita hujusmodi, larva barbaricae Latinitatis fucata, sed lectorem graviter distorquentia, et interdum ne ab Oedipo enucleanda, at diptherae tribuenda. Opere pretium existimabam quidpiam luminis in his accendere, et quod a doctis vel rejectum est, vel praetermissum, qualitercunque consarcinatum, exhibere. Ingentem vero ad hoc expeti animadverto apparatum: cognitionis, scientiae, lectionis, eruditionis, linguarum, judicii, otii, multorumque annorum tempestatem: claudum me in omnibus senemque elementarum in hanc arenam descendere, quis non rideret?

Page 48. Verstegen's book, *A Restitution of Decayed Intelligence* (Antwerp, 1605), is of unusual interest and worthy of further study.

Page 49. For the reference to the plans of D'Ewes see his *Autobiography and Correspondence,* ed. J. O. Halliwell, London, 1845, II. 4. For Dugdale's letter see *Life, Diary, and Correspondence,* ed. William Hamper, London, 1827, pp. 227 and 229.

Page 50. The quotation concerning the language is from

a *Prefatory Poem* for the dictionary, signed. Guliel. Jacob. Other etymological studies are as follows:

1663. Butler, Charles. *English Grammar,* containing a collection of Saxon and English words and a comparison of the two languages.

1671. Skinner, Stephen. *Etymologicon Anglicanum,* completed and published by Thos. Henshawe.

1675. Blount, Thomas. *Law Dictionary,* for the interpretation of old, difficult words.

1699. *Gazophylacum Anglicanum,* giving the derivation of English words both proper and common.

Page 51. Spelman's idea is given in the *Editoris Praefatio ad Lectorem* of the *Glossary:*

Sermone Saxonico nihil ei fuit antiquius, quippe qui optime noverat Saxonicam Linguam veram et genuinam esse Linguam *Anglicanam* adeo ut quantum a Saxonico vetere praesens *Anglicana* recesserit; tantum a nativa Puritate degeneraverit; et si quis vellet Verborum et Locutionum, quas quotidie usurpamus, Rationes et Proprietates intelligere, ad Saxonicas Origines necessario recurrendum esset.

Page 52. For the quotation from L'Isle see section 16. Steeves in his *Learned Societies* (New York, 1913) mentions the fact that four years after the Royal Society was founded a " Committee for Improving the English Tongue " was appointed. He adds (p. 41), " No record is extant of definite results attained by this committee, although it is certain that they held some formal meetings." As a matter of fact, John Wilkins, the leader of the committee, undertook a study of the language which appeared as *An Essay towards a Real Character and a Philosophical Language,* London, 1668. In the *Epistle Dedicatory* he appeals to the President of the Royal Society to " appoint some of our number thoroughly to examine and consider the whole " and to offer their criticism. He feels that this study is " rather the work of a College and an Age, then of any single Person." In this connection he suggests a

plan of coöperative research by which certain portions of the
larger subject would be investigated by various students. Some
such combined effort among graduate students might result in
a work of real importance. Wilkins offers an encouraging
thought for the research scholar in stating the value of minute
investigation. He says:

The discovery of the true nature and Cause of any the most minute
thing, doth promote real Knowledge, and therefore cannot be unfit
for any Man's endeavours, who is willing to contribute to the advancement of Learning.

Aubrey tells us (*Lives,* II. 302) that this study of the language
was Wilkins's " darling " and that " nothing troubled him so
much when he dyed, as that he had not completed it." Aubrey
also states that the work was being carried to completion by a
group of five, who would finish their work in about a year or
more. This undertaking of Wilkins may have been suggested
by Sir Thomas Urquhart's *Logopandecteision* (1653), a scheme
for a Universal language, in which he stated the idea that there
should be an analogy between things and words, and expressions for every possible conception of the mind.

    Page 56. The complete title of Slatyer's work is *Genethlia-
con, sive Stemma Iacobi: Genealogia scilicet Regia, Catholica,
Anglo, Scoto-Cambro-Britannica.* The quotation from Slatyer
is from the *Prefatory Poem* addressed *To the Maiestie of King
James.*

    Page 58. The references from Verstegen are found in
" The Epistle to Our Nation " and in the 1605 edition, pp.
94-5, respectively.

    Page 61. This debate concerning the true origin of the
nation is found chiefly in the historical and political writers of
the century. The writer of an anonymous *History of England*
(London, 1602 in *Harleian Miscellany,* II) " will not presume
. . . absolutely to contradict " the story of Brutus, though, he
adds, " for my own opinion, I suppose it to be a matter of more

antiquity, than verity "; and he begins his history with the Romans, " whence we have the first certain direction how to proceed." Howes, in continuing Stow, defends the Brutus story. He lists those who deny and those who support it, saying that those who dissent are the ones who base their opinions on conjecture, whereas those who uphold the story have the "Authority of so many ancient Authors, whereof most are very learned and sincere, and by all likelihood, had seen divers ancient writings and monuments " now extinct. He devotes a section, therefore, to " the authority and proofe, of *Brute* and *Troy.*" Edward Ayscu's *Historie* (London, 1607) holds that the story of the Trojans was " coyned in some Munkish mind about foure hundred yeares agone " (p. 1) and traces the British descent from the Gauls. Speed, *History of Great Britain* (London, 1611), gives an orderly summary of the arguments for and against the Trojan story, though he dismisses it by saying that if our nation must have its descent from the Trojans, this descent may be traced to the marriage of the British with the Romans after the Roman invasion. Even this he does not consider to be a high honor, for the Roman nation " stood only for six descents," it was " often vanquished " during that time, and it had its derivation from a bastard. As the other nations have cast off their " Demi-gods," he pleads with the English to " disclaime their Brute." He considers the early British " meerly barbarous," as he shows in his chapter on " The Manners and Customes of the Ancient Britaines "; but in telling of the uncivilized state, he points out that all nations have equally crude beginnings. The time before Caesar is dismissed with only a brief summary. Anthony Munday includes in his *A briefe Chronicle from the Creation to this time* (London, 1611) accounts of both Brutus and Arthur but does not vouch for their stories, attributing his material to " Mr. Lyte's *Light of Britain.*" Of the two unpublished historical manuscripts of this approximate period which are in the British Museum, *Harleian 2414* contains some of the fabulous British matter.

Drayton, in defending " the ancient and noble things " of England and preserving accounts of them from the destruction caused by time and indifference, supports the legend of Brute on the ground that the songs of the British bards are more reliable than books. The river Dee, therefore, repeats in the Tenth Song of the *Polyolbion* the story of the " Britain-founding Brute." Raleigh, on the other hand, will have nothing to do with these " monstrous originals " and begins his history with the certain facts of the time of William the Conqueror. Bolton in *Hypercritica* (1618) holds up the warning that if the legend of Brute be discarded " there is a vast Blanck upon the Times of our Country." He lines up the supporters and the opponents of Geoffrey, showing that those who were for him were greater in number than those who were against him; and though he recognizes much of Geoffrey as fabulous, yet he would have " so much of every Historical Monument or Historical Tradition maintain'd, as may well be holden without open absurdity." In spite of this theoretical defense of tradition, however, Bolton in practice begins his history with Caesar, writing *Nero Caesar or Monarchie Depraved* in 1624. Samuel Daniel, *Collection of the History of England* (London, 1612), follows Raleigh in the idea that the early times are uncertain and gives only a brief summary before William I. John Taylor includes the Brutus myth in both his *A Memoriall of all the English Monarchs, from Brute to King Charles* (London, 1630) and his shorter *The number and names of all the Kings of England and Scotland* (London, 1649), which he published for those who " cannot reach to " the " high rates " of the large Chronicles. The material is compiled from Boethius, Holinshed, Stow, Howes, and Middleton, and is presented without criticism in regard to the Trojan legend. The picture of each king is given, the main facts of his reign are told in rhyming couplets, and other facts are added in prose. Sir Richard Baker in his *Chronicle of the Kings of England* (London, 1641) admits that the stories of the ancient times are only fables "which may please children, but not riper Judgements." Edward Chamberlayne's *Angliae Notitia* (3d edition, 1669) is primarily concerned with the support of prerogative and matters of law, but gives a brief summary of the first inhabitants, rejecting the Trojan legend and deriving the nation from the Gauls. Philip Southby before 1657 discusses the whole question in a survey called *Brittaines Originall*. *Cambria Triumphans, or ancient and modern British and Welsh History from Brute to Charles I* (London, 1661) reveals in the title the attitude of the author, Pierce Enderby, and the purpose of the work in complimenting the British descent of Charles I. Milton sees in the early period a veritable storehouse for the poets and knowing that they will know how rightly to use it, he includes it for them. Prior, in defending the "Poeticall Authority" of the Trojan legend in the preface to his *Ode to the Queen*, cites the fact that the story was "told by Milton as if (at least) He was pleas'd with it." Prior adds, however, "Though possibly He does not believe it." Bulstrode Whitelocke in the *Memorials of the English Affairs from the Suppos'd Expedition of Brute to this Island, to the End of the Reign of King James the First* (London, 1709. Written before 1675) reveals in the wording of this long title his attitude toward legendary matter, which he nevertheless includes for whatever it may be worth.

In spite of the definite trend away from belief in the Trojan legend Silas Taylor in the *History of Gavelkind* (London, 1663) defends the story of Brutus, disparaging Polydore Virgil and upholding Geoffrey of Monmouth. Sheringham in *De Anglorum Gentis Origine Disceptatio* (Cambridge, 1670) set forth the entire dispute and took a positive stand for the Trojans. He concedes that there may be some fabulous material incorporated in the British story, but says that it is less than other nations are guilty of. He even goes so far as to claim that English law derives from the British, not the Saxons, and that the Saxons merely translated the British law into their own language. Daniel Langhorn's *Elenchus Antiquitatum Albionensium* (London, 1673) gives from Geoffrey a brief account of how Brute settled the kingdom and later divided it among his sons. He devotes considerable space to a discussion of the credibility of Geoffrey, citing those who confirm him. He concludes that Geoffrey inserted many fables, so that truth is mixed with myth. George Meriton in *Anglorum Gesta* (London, 1675) discredits Geoffrey's account of the settlement by Brute by saying that the ancient historians tell nothing of any such person. He feels, however, that " there is no Book so bad, even sir Bevise himselfe, Fryer Bacon, or Tom Thumb, but some advantage may be gotten by it," and with such charity he looks upon Geoffrey. The *Divi Britannica* (London, 1675) by Winston Churchill offers the opinion that though all the records of early times are untrustworthy, the lack of chronology should not cause one to " blow off sixty Kings at one blast." Aylett Sammes in the *Antiquities of Ancient Britain* (London, 1676) terms the Trojan story fabulous and sees no certainty in Geoffrey's chronology, a source which he considers unworthy. Stillingfleet in *Origines Britannicae* (London, 1685) says, " Some Mens Eyes are still so tender as not to be able to beare the strong impressions of Light; especially in what relates to the Antiquities of thir own Countrey " (*Preface,* pp. 1-2). He turns the light, nevertheless, directly upon these traditions: the Trojan legend is only a conventional type of origin common to all nations in imitation of the Romans; this convention is one that is used to appeal to those who love a show of learning, but it hardly passes with those of judgment anywhere; there are, however, many " who were better pleased with the Particulars of Legend than the dryness of true History "; it is these particulars which especially cast doubt upon the early material, for oral tradition may preserve the outstanding events but not the details. John Heath in *England's Chronicles* (London, 1691) agrees that the derivation from Brutus is not plausible and begins his history with the time of Caesar. *A History of Britan* printed for R. Cheswell in 1695, however, begins with the " first Traditional Beginning." Nathaniel Crouch, writing under the pseudonym of Richard Burton, expresses doubt of the Brutus story in his *History of the Principality of Wales* (London, 1695) ; and William Nicolson in the *Historical Library,* the first volume of which was published in 1696, gives as his opinion that there is as much truth in the Brutus origin as in mythological tales. " Many learned men," says Nicolson, have attempted to establish the Arthurian part of the story on account of its importance to history. He quotes, therefore, from the defenders of Geoffrey, but gives (p. 37 of the 3rd edition, 1736) as his own opinion:

I am not for *wholly rejecting* all that's contain'd in that History, believing there is somewhat of Truth in it, under a mighty Heap of Monkish Forgeries.

Sir William Temple, *History of England* (London, 1695), holds the view that not only is the period before Caesar " cover'd with the Rust of Time," but that fables have been " forged at Pleasure by the Wit or Folly of their first Authors, and [are] not to be regarded." The Saxons, on the other hand, had authors less " *Few* and *Mean* " than often supposed, as he establishes by very good proof. William Wynne in 1697 improves Dr. Powel's translation of Caradoc's *History of Wales* and in a long preface defends the period from Brute to Cadwallader which, he says, " has been generally accounted of late, absolutely false and unhistorical." Though he admits that Geoffrey is probably not " universally true," yet he says his material is not " so absolutely fabulous as is frequently represented and generally believed." His defense of Geoffrey is an interesting one. Parts of Newburgh, the first detractor, are false; early testimony is favorable; Matthew Paris calls Geoffrey a " faithful translator of the British history "; if Geoffrey were a cheat, he could best have been discovered in those times; if he were inventing, he would not diverge so widely from Roman historians, " for certainly, nothing could add more authority to a fable, than exactly to follow the steps of creditable authors, in those things they both had occasion to treat of "; furthermore, he would not have dared dedicate his book to Henry I and Robert of Gloucester, for he might have been discovered and thereby ruined. Wynne then cites Sheringham's defense and concludes by accepting the entire Geoffrey story. James Tyrrel at the end of the century takes an entirely different stand. He speaks in his *General History of England* (London, 1700) of " the exploded fables of Geoffrey of Monmouth." He thinks that Sammes gives too much credit to Geoffrey, but he himself, while drawing from Geoffrey for the legends which he holds it " sometimes of Advantage to know," says he would not include them " if it had not been more for the Diversion of the younger sort of Readers, and that the Work would have been thought by some others imperfect without it " (*Preface to the Reader,* p. vii).

To the end of the century, therefore, we see the continuation of the conflict beteen British and Saxon. This struggle is closely bound up with the struggle between the Parliament and the king, and the interest fluctuates from Saxon to British according to which of these forces has the greater power.

Page 63. Contemporary investigation presents remarkable evidence in support of Geoffrey's account. Both Miss Winstanley, " Science and the Celtic Tradition," in the *Welsh Outlook,* 4 (1917) pp. 237-9, and H. J. Fleure, *The Races of England and Wales,* London, 1923, have made discoveries concerning the Trojan migrations and have connected these with the facts given by Geoffrey. Other corroborating material is found in L. A. Waddell's *Phoenician Origin of Britans, Scots, and Anglo-Saxons,* London, 1924. In his general line of defense of the Geoffrey story and his presentation of the latest archeological discoveries, which seem to authenticate important sections of Geoffrey's account, Acton Griscom, *Historia Regum Britanniae* (New York, 1929) has made an extremely important contribution toward establishing the general dependability of Geoffrey's account. In this connection it is interesting to note that with the exception of the recent archeological discoveries, the first English translation of the *Historia* (1718) by Aaron Thompson presents the same lines of defense as Griscom's *Historia:* the learning and reputation of Geoffrey; the early unquestioning acceptance by reputable scholars when there were "more monuments extant" and traditions were fresher; the attack of Newburgh attributable to a "revenge he thought he owed the Welsh for an affront they had given him"; the continued credit of Geoffrey after this attack; and the confirmation of Welsh manuscripts, to which he directs the attention of other scholars, since he was unable to translate Welsh. In the light of modern scholarship it would seem that the seventeenth century defenders of Geoffrey, though they reached their conclusions on less tenable grounds than those offered by modern scholars, were in the main, right.

These reports by various members of the Society of Antiquaries are to be found in Thomas Hearne's *A Collection of Curious Discourses,* London, 1775, I. 168, 213, 221, 227, 239, 314-5, etc.

Page 69. Arthurian matter in *England's Heroical Epistles* is found in Mortimer's *Epistle to Queen Isabel,* Queen Catherine's *Epistle to Owen Tudor,* and Owen Tudor's reply.

Page 77. It is interesting to compare the abasement of Merlin, which took place in France somewhat later, although this decline in reputation is largely due to the influence of

Cervantes' *Don Quixote* and takes a very different expression from that seen in England. Guérin de Bouscal in his *Don Quichot de la Manche,* Second partie (1640), represents Merlin as entering in ballet style with several others and saying:

> Ie ne resiste pas
> A monstrer, plus enfant du Diable,
> Ny ce grand Enchanteur dont on fait tant de cas:
> Et qui vent sur ce poinct en scavoir davantage,
> Consulte mon visage.

The " Chavaliers de la Table-Ronde " were used in ballet also about 1643. An account of this ballet, called *Le Libraire du Pont-Neuf ou les romans,* is in Paul Lacroix's *Ballets et Mascarades,* VI. 59 ff. Guérin's play reworked by Mlle. Béjart into a comedy entitled *D. Quichot ou les Enchantements de Merlin* was played by Molière's troupe on January 30 and February 1 and 3, 1660. Several other Merlin plays seem to have been popular. *Les Amours de Merlin,* a comedy in one act in verse by Rosidor, was played in Rouen in 1671. *Merlin peintre,* attributed to Thuellerie, was presented at the Comédie Française July 20, 1687, but was not printed. Two other plays said to have been acted with success but not printed were *Merlin Gascon* by Raisin l'aîné, given in the Théâtre Français on October 7, 1690, and *Merlin déserteur,* attributed to Dancourt and acted at his theatre on August 28, 1690. An amusing confusion has arisen concerning Desmarres' *La Dragonne, ou Merlin Dragon* of 1696. In this play *dragon* means *dragoon* and not *dragon!* Merlin has no association with the Arthurian character, but is only a valet disguised as Captain of the dragoons for purposes of intrigue. The *British Museum Catalogue* lists this play with the literature associated with the prophet Merlin, and A. E. Curdy classifies it as Arthurian in his "Arthurian Literature " in the *Romanic Review,* July-Sept., 1910. I am indebted to Professor Carrington Lancaster for clearing up this point by reference to frères Parfaict, *Histoire du Théâtre Français* (1748) XIII. 18-21. Professor Lancaster has very generously given me other French references. I am also indebted to Dr. Esther Crooks for her coöperation in securing the above material, which suggests an interesting field for future more detailed study.

Page 82. The quotations from Sammes, *Antiquities of Ancient Britain,* are from pp. 159 and 400, respectively, of the edition of 1676. The quotation from Stillingfleet is from p. 334 of the 1685 edition; that from Nicolson is p. 37 of the 1736 edition.

FOR CHAPTER III

Page 89. M. W. MacCallum, in *Tennyson's Idylls of the King and Arthurian Story from the XVIth Century* (Glasgow, 1894), p. 125, also discusses Shakespeare's use of Arthurian material.

Page 90. For a good discussion of Shakespeare and the Welsh see *Shakespeare and His Welsh Characters* by A. E. Hughes, London, 1922.

Page 91. *Fuimus Troes* is in Dodsley's *Old Plays* (1825-35), VII. The reference to Wood (p. 92) is to *Athen. Oxon.,* I. 619.

Page 95. The story of Brute is found in the Fourth Song of Book II of *Britannia's Pastorals.*

Page 96. For an account of the Elizabethan band of Arthur's knights see C. B. Millican's "Spenser and the Arthurian Legend," in *RES,* April, 1930.

Page 101. This correspondence is in *C. S. P. Dom. Charles I,* 1636-7, p. 379.

Page 102. The quotation from Cowley is from *A Poem on the Civil War Begun in the Year 1641.*

Page 104. The minor references to Arthur scattered through the literature of the period are scarcely more significant than mythological references: see, for example, Denham's allusion to the builders of Windsor in *Cooper's Hill* (1643) ; Waller's reference to " Fair Arthur's shield " in his *In Answer to One who writ against a Fair Lady:* Chamberlayne's mention of the Knight and the Lady of the Lake in *Love's Victory;* Cleveland's decree that Sir Thomas Martin should be " Voider to King Arthur's Table " in his *Upon Sir Thomas Martin;* Richard Corbet's boast that he could sing the ballad of Arthur; Wither's mention of Winchester as the place of Arthur's Court in *Mistress Philarete;* Sir Thomas Browne's account of the unearthing of Arthur's bones at Glastonbury in *Hydriotaphia;* and like references.   Deloney's ballad was reprinted in 1650, but so was *The Shepherd and the King,* a ballad about Alfred.

Page 108.   Photostats of both Jegon's *A Supplement of the Faery Queene* and Sheppard's *The Faerie King* were secured by the Tudor and Stuart Club of the Johns Hopkins University in 1930 for use in this study and in the Spenser study being carried on at the University.

Page 118.   I do not mean to imply, of course, that Crouch was giving Arthur a new position, but to indicate the line of his defense of the historicity of Arthur against the questioning attitude of contemporary writers.

FOR CHAPTER IV

Page 124.   This quotation from Jonson is from the *Conversations,* Herford and Simpson edition of Jonson's *Works,* I. 132.

Page 130.   The idea that Milton would not use Arthurian matter because it was not true was restated in an article in *PMLA* (1927), by R. F. Jones, entitled " Milton and the Epic Subject from British History."   Hanford's opinion is stated in the " Chronology of Milton's Private Studies," in *SP,* XXXVI (1921), p. 299.

Page 131.   The quotation from Milton's *History of Britain* is from the edition of 1677, p. 144.   This is the edition used throughout this study except for the parallel beginning Book III, which is not in the 2nd edition.

Page 136. E. M. W. Tillyard in his *Milton* (London and New York, 1930) suggests that there is a connection between Milton's study of British historical material and his desire to write an epic which would express the Commonwealth. He explains the abandonment of the historical material on the ground that Milton came to feel that "his country's leaders" were not "worth celebrating in his writings any more" (p. 177). *The History of Britain,* he says, is the result of these abandoned researches, and *Paradise Lost* the theme to which Milton turned in his disappointment. Acceptance of the theory that the subject of *Paradise Lost* was chosen as the expression of contemporary life relieves one of the dual view expressed by Tillyard in the "conscious meaning" and the "unconscious meaning" of *Paradise Lost* and strengthens the idea that there is "one broad general meaning to the poem," an idea which Tillyard finds it difficult to accept (p. 295. See also pp. 258 ff.). The fact that Dryden (greatly influenced as he was by Milton) represented Arthur in the temptation to passion as looking upon reason as a "load of life" and deliberately choosing to throw off this load, strengthens the conclusion that Milton was depicting the struggle between passion and rational control. Blackmore, writing under the influence of Spenser, Milton, and Dryden, portrays this same conflict. It is interesting to note that the analysis of the allegory of Aurelian Townshend's *Tempe Restor'd,* 1631, explains one scene as showing the "Harmony of the Irascible and concupiscible parts obedient to the rationall and highest part of the soule."

In connection with Milton's parallel between his own age and the British period we should keep in mind the plan of Sir Simonds D'Ewes. He writes on May 5, 1628 (*Autobiography,* I. 374) that he began a book entitled *Great Britains Strength and Weakness* in which he intended to parallel the dangers of

his own day with the " dangers of former ages " in order to
throw light upon the present and to show " how both Church
and State might yet be upheld." When the meeting of Parliament came to nought in June, he discontinued his work, for,
he says, " I thought my labour would be too full of truth and
plainness to endure the public view of the world." He had
written some parts of the intended book, and these are preserved in the Harleian manuscripts. He felt recompensed for
his study because of both his own gain in knowledge and the
collection of material for a *History of Britain* which he had
determined to write and was gathering notes for as early as
1620 when he was at Cambridge (I. 140). Like Milton,
D'Ewes dedicated his work to the " public good, not doubting,
if God sent me life, but to leave somewhat to posterity." He
began serious work, studying Aristotle, collecting notes from
Florus's *Roman History,* imitating Aulus, Gellius, Fronto, and
Corsellius Vindex, and translating Horace. For recreation at
night he read " Stephens' Apology for Herodotus, or Spencer's
Fairie Queen."

Page 142. For the reference to Dryden see Scott and
Saintsbury, Dryden's *Works,* Edinburgh, 1821, XIII. 26-30.

Page 146. The most recent study of Blackmore is T. N.
Toomey's " Sir Richard Blackmore," in *Annals of Medical
History,* t. 4 (1922), pp. 180-88. This assembles the chief
facts of Blackmore's life, adding some definite dates from old
records, and gives a good bibliography.

Blackmore is best known for his philosophical poem, *The
Creation* (1712). This is far superior to his epics, for in
the latter he wrote profusely without taking time to polish his
work, so that we are lost frequently in a flow of words which
move along in inflated heroic couplets. In addition to his two
Arthurian epics he wrote *Eliza* (1705), figuring under the
time of Queen Elizabeth events of the reign of Queen Anne,
and *Alfred* (1723), dedicated to Prince Frederick.

Blackmore belonged to the group which considered that the chief aim of poetry was to teach. In the *Lay Monastery*, a group of essays in two volumes, continuing the *Spectator* (1713-4), p. 188, he says that it is the purpose of both heroic painting and epic poetry " not only to move the Passions, but to inspire generous Sentiments and convey to the Mind Moral and Divine Instruction." In the *Preface* to *Prince Arthur* he describes the " true and genuine End " of poetry as " the Instruction of our Minds, and Regulation of our Manners." He has a high regard for the power of poetry in shaping life and feels that it may " touch any Spring that moves the Heart," or that it may " agitate the Soul with any sort of Affection." He points out the service of tragedy, comedy, and satire in " the Promotion of Virtue, and exposing of Vice "; the purpose of the ode in exciting men to imitation of the gods and heroes; and the aim of epic poetry to teach virtue. The seriousness of all poetry is summed up in the statement:

To give Men right and just Conceptions of Religion and Virtue, to aid their Reason in restraining their Exhorbitant Appetites and Impetuous Passions, and to bring their Lives under the Rules and Guidance of true Wisdom, and thereby to promote the Publick Good of Mankind, is undoubtedly the End of all Poetry.

He, therefore, in both *Prince Arthur* and *King Arthur* deplores the misuse of poetry and especially attacks the comedy of his own day on the ground that it popularizes vice and ridicules religion. Blackmore's concern over the depravity of taste in his period is shown by the fact that he left reversionary interest on £1000 to encourage a student every year to write a poem of 650 lines on " a Divine Subject " and prose pamphlets " against the obscene plays and publications of the time " (Cunningham, *Lives,* II. 265). Quarles and Milton had also expressed their reaction against the prevailing taste with much the same bitterness. Quarles (*Preface to the Reader,* in *Hadassa,* II. 42) says, " In these lewd times, the salt, and soule of a Verse, is obscene scurrility." Milton deplores the "corruption and bane" which the youth "suck in daily from the writings and interludes of libidinous and ignorant poetasters," saying that "vicious principles" are hidden in "sweet pills" (*Reason of Church Government*). One of the purposes of Blackmore in writing *Prince Arthur* is to rescue "the Muses out of the Hands of these Ravishers, to restore them to their sweet and chast Mansions." In the *Preface* to *King Arthur* he does praise the *Mourning Bride* and argues that it refutes the claim of other dramatists that the "degenerate age" made the portrayal of loose morals necessary to success. Blackmore's *Alfred*, as well as the Arthurian epics, was written for moral instruction. In this connection it is interesting to note that as in the case of King Arthur the supreme temptation is to allow passion to dominate reason.

Page 149. Oskar Liis in his dissertation (Strassburg, 1911), *Die Arthurepen des Sir Richard Blackmore*, has made a very detailed comparison of Blackmore's lines with those of the *Aeneid* and of *Paradise Lost*. Many of his parallels with both works seem quite strained, but the cumulative impression of influence is great. The comparison of figures of speech is pushed entirely too far. In the meticulous presentation of details, Liis loses sight of the larger pattern and the more significant likeness of ideas.

Page 155. The qualities of the ruler as pointed out by Aristotle are given in Jowett's translation of the *Politics*, I. 1254-60.

Page 156. For the discussion of the *Arcadia* I am indebted to Professor Edwin Greenlaw's "Sidney's *Arcadia* as Elizabethan Allegory" in *Kittredge Anniversary Papers*, Boston, 1913, pp. 327 ff.

The quotation from the *Arcadia* is from Albert Feuillerat's edition of Sidney's *Works*, Cambridge, 1922, I. 77. Jonson's remark is in the *Conversations*. I am quoting from J. E.

Spingarn's *Critical Essays of the Seventeenth Century,* Oxford, 1908-9, I. 213.

Page 157. The analysis of the temptation of both Guyon and Adam is in Greenlaw's " A Better Teacher than Aquinas " in *SP,* XIV (1917).

Page 164. Milton's influence on Blackmore has been noted by Howard Maynadier, *The Arthur of the English Poets,* New York, 1907 (especially p. 299) ; Raymond D. Havens, The *Influence of Milton on English Poetry,* Harvard University Press, 1922 (especially p. 91) ; and Oskar Liis, *Die Arthurepen des Sir Richard Blackmore.*

Page 166. The quotation from Boileau is from *The Art of Poetry,* ed. David Nichol Smith, Cambridge, 1907, Chant Troisième, 199-204.

Page 168. The reference is to *Essays upon Several Subjects,* 1716-7, I. 43.

Page 178. Nicholas Rowe made a similar identification of William with an historical character when he portrayed him in drama as Tamerlane and pictured his enemy, Louis XIV, as Bajazet.

Page 183. Blackmore's suggestions for an epic on Marlborough are in *Advice to the Poets.*

Page 187. For the reference to Molyneux see Hill's edition of Jonson's *Lives,* II. 238, note 2. For the statement of Locke see *Works,* 1812, p. 568.

Pages 188-90. The reference to Covent Garden is, of course, to Will's Coffee House, where Dryden presided over the poets and critics, and the so called " coffee-critics " made or ruined many a reputation. Moyle in a letter to Congreve regrets that he could not be present at the initiation of a new poet into the society of Covent Garden and says:

Would to God I could Laugh with you, for one hour or two, at all the ridiculous things that have happen'd at *Will's* Coffee-house since I left it; 'tis the merriest place in the world.

The references to Dryden are to be found in *Preface to the Fables, Works,* ed. Scott and Saintsbury, XI. 241-2. The remarks about Blackmore's degrees and the ridicule of Maurus are in *Works,* VIII. 482-4 and XI. 76, respectively. Pope's criticism is to be found in *Works,* ed. Elvin and Courthope, X. 360 and 207; *Imitations of Horace, Epistle I.* 16 and II. 386; *Satires* II. 23; *Dunciad* II. 302 (also minor references: I. 104, II. 259-68, and 370). Swift's examples of *Bathos* are in *Works,* ed. Scott (1741) XIII. The passage on Lucan and Blackmore is p. 162 of the Everyman edition of *The Battle of the Books.* Gay (*English Poets,* XXXVI. 302) indulged in some " Verses to be placed under the Picture of England's Arch-Poet (Sir Richard Blackmore)." This contains a list of Blackmore's works given in a satirical manner and devises various types of punishment for Blackmore, reaching a climax in the prayer that he be sent the wife of Job. Garth's ridicule is in the *Dispensary,* IV. 172, 203. Though Addison praises Blackmore's *Creation* (*Spectator,* 339), and his *Essays* (*Freeholder,* no. 45), he slurs at Blackmore's muse " that could make a couple of heroic poems in a hackney coach and a coffee house " (Letter from Amsterdam, Sept. 7, 1703, in Aikin's *Addison,* I. 161), and is said by Swift to have despised Blackmore (Notes on Addison's *Freeholder* in Swift's *Works,* ed. Scott, XII. 132).

The battle of the critics extended beyond the limits of the century, but in spite of all this hostility Blackmore was implored to celebrate the victory at Brabant (*An Epistle to Sir Richard Blackmore, Kt. On occasion of the late great Victory in Brabant,* London, 1706). Though he refused to undertake the subject, he sketched a plan for its treatment, advising the *Iliad* and the *Aeneid* as models and advocating Christian machinery and the allegorical method. The critics replied with an anonymous parody (1708) entitled *The Flight of the Pretender with Advice to the Poets. A Poem in the*

Arthurical . . . Jobical . . . Elizabethical Style and Phrase of the sublime Poet Maurus. Blackmore answered with *Instructions to Vanderbank* (1709), which in turn was ridiculed by Steele in the *Tatler.* After this the matter dropped.

More interesting than Dennis's criticism of *Prince Arthur* is the outline which Dennis makes for an anticipated work on poetical genius. It is his intention first to analyze genius as the transport which follows the consciousness of an excellence arising from the " conception of an extraordinary hint." The effect is the same as that of " happiness in common Life." Hints that may transport are " hints of thoughts " and " hints of images." It was his plan to illustrate images of " sounds or of things" from Homer, Virgil, Tasso, and Milton. After considering images, he intends to discuss diction, analyzing the difference between poetic diction and the diction of prose, and making a study of " our English numbers, and of our Rhymes and Cadences." Had he taken up the question of diction, he would have entered upon a point which had been engrossing much attention since about the middle of the century, especially through French influence. The *Pleiade* had ruled out the use of all humble words and mechanical or scientific terms, and Le Moyne in the preface to *St. Louis,* all low, vulgar, and plebeian terms. In England Davenant accepted words from science and the mechanical arts, though not low words. Hobbes replied to Davenant, siding with the French and advocating also the omission of all words too old or too new in use. Dryden followed the *Pleiade* (see preface to *Annus Mirabilis*). Blackmore thought that the diction should be above " the vulgar Manner of Speech and Expression " and that a " sublime style " should be used to " raise and embellish " the greater part of an epic poem; the style, however, must always suit the matter treated. When the subject does not demand a lofty diction, its use would " appear as contemptible and ridiculous as a Peasant clad in Robes of State " (preface to *Alfred,* xxxix).

He cites examples of low and flat style in Virgil, Lucretius, and Milton. In giving his *Advice to the Poets*, Blackmore inveighs against the imitators of the elevated style of Milton:

> No more let Milton's Imitators dare
> Torture our Language, to torment our Ear
> With numbers harsher than the din of war.

He recommends adornment, but it is to be a combination from the classics and Spenser:

> Let Mantuan Judgment, and Horatian Words,
> And all the noble Fire which *Greece* affords,
> With all the Beauties which in Spencer shine,
> To form their Diction's Dignity combine.

The change from the above point of view to that of Wordsworth is another chapter of considerable interest in literary history.

INDEX OF AUTHORS